VIRGINIA.

OVERWHARTON PARISH REGISTER,
1720 to 1760.

OLD STAFFORD COUNTY.

BY

WM. F. BOOGHER.

Notice

In many older books, foxing (or discoloration) occurs and, in some instances, print lightens with wear and age. Reprinted books, such as this, often duplicate these flaws, notwithstanding efforts to reduce or eliminate them. The pages of this reprint have been digitally enhanced and, where possible, the flaws eliminated in order to provide clarity of content and a pleasant reading experience.

Originally published
Washington D. C.
1899

Reprinted by:

Janaway Publishing, Inc.
732 Kelsey Ct.
Santa Maria, California 93454
(805) 925-1038
www.janawaygenealogy.com

2006, 2011

ISBN 10: 1-59641-022-1
ISBN 13: 978-1-59641-022-0

Made in the United States of America

CONTENTS.

HISTORICAL SKETCH OF THE COUNTY OF STAFFORD,

AND

THE PARISH OF OVERWHARTON.

VIEWS OF AQUIA CHURCH, ETC.

1856-1899.

Preface.

STAFFORD COUNTY, VIRGINIA.

THE County of Stafford and Parish of Overwharton derive their names from the corresponding ones in England. The County of Stafford was erected in 1666 out of Westmoreland, extending to the Blue Ridge Mountains, being the frontier county, and was about twenty-four miles in width south and west of the Potomac River. It was first represented in the House of Burgesses by Col. Henry Mees, June, 1666. (Henings Statutes, Vol. 2, p. 250,) he being allowed 130 lbs. of tobacco and a cask per day; traveling expenses at the rate of four days each way for his attendance as a member of the Assembly. If traveling by water, only 120 lbs. of tobacco per day. (Mercer's

Abridgment, p. 39.) The county first appears among the proceedings of the Assembly as a county in June, 1675, when with Rappahannock, Westmoreland and Northumberland, Stafford was exempted from erecting looms and weaves, in consideration of the newness of the soil and the consequent inability to maintain them; this being more conducive proof of its establishment as a county than the mere circumstance of its being represented in the Assembly, as by the law then existing, any county which would lay out 100 acres of land and people it with 100 tithable persons should be entitled to a representative in the Assembly, notwithstanding the Act limiting the number to two representatives for a county. (Hening, Vol. 2, pp. 238-9.)

This law was changed October, 1705, requiring 800 tithable persons necessary to erect a new County on the frontier. Stafford Court House was first built at Marlboro, on the Potomac, afterwards moved about 100 yards from the site of the present Court House, which was built in 1783—material, brick covered with stucco of mortar; main building 20x40, with a T wing 20x30; two acres of land for Court House and Prison deeded in 1783 by William Gerrard and William Fitzhugh. The number of voters in the County in 1899 was 1725; 1400 white and 325 colored. Population of the village of Stafford Court House is 25, all white.

There are but few records of old Stafford County to

be found in the vault of this ancient Court House until about 1699. Very many of those from 1699 to 1862 were either destroyed or stolen during the civil war. Those that remain are indexed so that examiners have no trouble in searching.

For the names of the Justices of the County from 1666 to 1860, see Vol. 2, p. 206, "Old Churches and Families," by Bishop Meade; from 1860 to 1899, we find, Edward Waller, 1860 to 1862; period of the war, '62 to '65———; N. W. Ford, 1865 to 1869; Charles Tankerly and John R. Evans, 1869; B. H. Hewitt, 1870. J. B. Jett, Judge of County Court, 1870 to 1874; J. B T. Suttle, 1874 to 1880; E. C. S. Hunter, 1880 to 1886; Charles H. Ashton, 1886 to 1898; R. H. L. Chichester, 1898 to 1899.—*Supplied by Mr. C. A. Bryan, Clerk of the Court.*

OVERWHARTON PARISH.

THIS Parish was co-extensive with Stafford County, covering a part of what was once Washington Parish, extending about eighty miles along the Potomac, in breadth about four and twenty miles, embracing within its territory what is now Prince William, Loudoun, Fairfax, Alexandria Counties and a part of Fauquier until 1730, when Prince William County was taken from Stafford, and Hamilton Parish was erected, succeeding Overwharton as the frontier parish. Of the early history of Overwharton Parish and its rectors, but little is known.

In 1724, there were 650 families and about 100 communicants. One church, Potomac (situated about nine miles south of the present Aquia Church), the brick walls of which were standing until torn down by the Federal army during the Civil War. It is, however, evident, from the number of white occupants of the soil within an area of ten miles, that there must have been frontier chapels of ease in the immediate locality of Potomac Church about 1675, if not a church. The Glebe Lands were within two miles of Potomac Church. The Rev. Dr. Scott was rector as early as 1710, and so continued until he died, April 1, 1738, aged 52 years, 9 months, and 20 days; he was succeeded by Rev. John Moncure, a Scotch gentleman, but of Huguenot descent, who acted as assistant or curator to the Rev. Mr. Scott for a short time previous to his death; Rev. Mr. Moncure continued as rector of the Parish until his death, in 1764. Of the old Potomac Church, there are no vestry records known to exist. The earliest records of members of the vestry of Overwharton Parish are those of Aquia Church, beginning in 1757. This church was first built in 1751, thirteen years after the death of Mr. Scott, and was destroyed by fire in 1754, and rebuilt in 1757 upon the original foundation, as charred remains are yet to be found under the church, and about the foundation.

An inscription over the door states as follows:

"Built 1751; destroyed by fire 1754*; rebuilt 1757."

And upon a panel on the gallery appears the following:

"John MONCURE, *Minister*, 1757.

VESTRYMEN:

PETER HEDGMAN,	BENJAMIN STROTHER,
JOHN MERCER,	THOS. FITZHUGH,
JOHN LEE,	PETER DANIEL, *Warden*,
MAT DONIPHAN,	TRAVERS COOK, *Warden*,
HENRY TYLER,	JOHN FITZHUGH,
WILLIAM MOUNTJOY,	JOHN PEYTON."

*Meade says burned in 1751; in this he is in error as Mr. Powhatan Moncure gives the record from the church door.

As to the successor of Mr. Moncure in this parish, it is probable that the Rev. Mr. Green took his place in 1764. In the years 1774 and 1776, the Rev. Clement Brooke was minister. After the Revolution, in the Convention of 1785, called for organizing the diocese and considering the question of a general confederation of Episcopalians throughout the Union, we find the Rev. Robert Buchan the minister of Overwharton parish, and the Rev. Mr. Thornton, of Brunswick parish, which had been taken from King George and given to Stafford when St. Paul's was taken from Stafford and given to King George. The lay delegates at that Convention were Mr. Charles Carter, representing Overwharton parish, and Mr. William Fitzhugh, of Chatham, representing Brunswick parish, and Mr. William Fitzhugh, of Chatham, representing Brunswick parish, which lay on the Rappahannock, and extended to Hanover parish in King George. In the year 1786, Mr. Fitzhugh again represented Brunswick parish; and this is the last notice we have of the Church in Stafford until some years after the revival of conventions. In the year 1819, the Rev. Thomas Allen took charge of this parish, preaching alternately at Dumfries and Aquia churches.* At a subsequent period the Rev. Mr. Prestman, gave all his energies to the work of its revival. The labors

---

*Mr. Allen took charge 1814; continued until 1823.—Pub.

of both were of some avail to preserve it from utter extinction, but not to raise it to anything like prosperity. The Rev. Mr. Johnson also made some inefectual efforts in its behalf as a missionary.

Old Aquia Church stands upon a high eminence, not very far from the main road from Alexandria to Fredericksburg. In 1838 it was a melancholy sight to behold the vacant space around the house, which in other days had been filled with horses and carriages and footmen, now overgrown with trees and bushes, the limbs of the green cedars not only casting their shadows but resting their arms on the dingy walls and thrusting them through the broken windows, thus giving an air of pensiveness and gloom to the whole scene. The very pathway up the commanding eminence on which it stood was filled with young trees, while the arms of the older ones so embraced each other over it that it was difficult to ascend. The church has a noble exterior, being a high two-story house, of the figure of the cross. On its top was an observatory, which was reached by a flight of stairs leading from the gallery, and from which the Potomac and Rappahannock Rivers, which are not far distant from each other, and much of the surrounding country, might be seen.

After a visit made to the same church, about 1856, Bishop Meade says:

"I should not have recognized the place or building. The trees, brushwood and rubbish had been cleared away. The light of heaven had been let in upon the once gloomy sanctuary. At the expense of eighteen hundred dollars (almost all of it contributed by the descendants of Mr. Moncure), the house had been repaired within, without and above. The dingy walls were painted white and looked new and fresh, and to me it appeared one of the best and most imposing temples in our land. The congregation was a good one. The descendants of Mr. Moncure, still bearing his name, formed a large portion."

The following is the view of the church subsequent to the late Civil War, supplied by Messrs. Lippincott & Co., being from the same plate as the one used in "Old Churches and Families of Virginia," by Bishop Meade, Vol. 2, pp. 197–206, to which publication I am indebted for a portion of this historical sketch.

About 1840 the church had fallen into decay and remained so, as stated by Bishop Meade, until about 1850, when the Rev. Henry Wall took charge as minister. He was succeeded about 1858 by the Rev. Mr. Mackenheimer, who serve until the Civil War, during which time the church was temporarily occupied by the Federal troops and, as a result was desecrated and defaced, for which a claim is now pending before Congress.

AOQUIA CHURCH, STAFFORD CO., VA.

Shortly after the war the church was again repaired, largely by the assistance of Rev. J. M. Meredith and Hon. Wm. S. Scott, of Pennsylvania, a descendant of Rev. Alexander Scott. Rev. Mr. Meredith then became rector, and in 1875 was succeeded by Rev. Mr. Appleton; in 1877 by Mr. Pruden; in 1878 Rev. Geo. M. Funsten; in 1884 by Rev. Thos. Carter Page, who remained until 1889. It was then vacant for two years, when Rev. John H. Birckhead became rector and remained until 1896. He was succeeded by the present incumbent, Rev. J. Howard Gibbons. The above dates are claimed to be nearly exact. Vestrymen before the war, not known, but the first vestry after was as follows:

Gen. FITZHUGH LEE	GEO. V. MONCURE,
WM. E. MONCURE, *Warden.*	HUGH ADIE,
R. C. L. MONCURE, *Warden.*	N. W. FORD,
POWHATAN MONCURE,	E. A. W. HORE,
Col. THOMAS WALLER,	BENJAMIN A. BELL.

The present vestry is as follows, viz:

JAS. ASHBY,	WALTER BOZZELL, *Sec'y and Treas*
POWHATAN MONCURE,	
HUGH ADIE,	E. D. MONCURE,
GEO. V. MONCURE, JR.,	FRANK BLACKBURN,
R. C. L. MONCURE, SR.,	R. MINOR MONCURE,
J. M. ASHBY,	WM. P. PATTERSON.
R. A. MONCURE,	

Number of families represented, not known. Present number of communicants, 80.

WM. F. BOOGHER.

To the courtesy of Mr. P. Moncure I am indebted for the following illustrations of the Exterior and Interior Views of this old historical Church, as it is at present.

EXTERIOR VIEW AQUIA CHURCH, 1899.

INTERIOR VIEW AQUIA CHURCH, 1899.

Overwharton Parish Register,

1720 to 1750.

A.

Aldrige, John. Married Annie Hamilton,
June 11, 1738
Abram, Mary. Married Walter Morgan Lewis,
August 27, 1738
Allen, William. Departed this life January 13, 1741
Asbee, Elizabeth. Daughter of Jean and John, born
July 9, 1742
Asbee, Stephen. Son of Robert and Mary, born
October 19, 1742
Atchison, Adam. Married Elizabeth Byram,
October 20, 1742
Allentrop, Jacob. Son of John and Annie, baptized
December 24, 1742
Allen, William. Married Bridget Withers,
February 15, 1743
Allen, John. Son of Archibald and Abigail, born
August 12, 1743

Allen, Margaret. Departed this life September 1, 1743
Allen, James. Son of William and Bridget, born
January 2, 1744
Atchison, Mary. Daughter of Adam and Betty, born
April 11, 1744
Asbee, Stephen. Son of Robert and Mary, died
September 5, 1744
Asbee, Ann. Daughter of Robert and Mary, born
January 10, 1745
Ashby, Elias. Married Winifred Million,
September 4, 1745
Asberry, John. Married Jean Boalin,
February 25, 1745
Adams, George. Died the first day of March, 1745
Angell, Samuel. Married Ann Hornbuckle,
August 14, 1745
Atchison, John. Son of Adam and Elizabeth, born
January 9, 1746
Asbee, William. Son of Elias and Winifred, born
April 23, 1746
Allen, Elizabeth. Daughter of Bridget and William,
born April 26, 1746
Allenthrop, Benjamin. Married Elizabeth Fletcher,
August 19, 1746
Angel, Jannett. Born at William Black's,
December 29, 1746

Asbee, Sarah. Daughter of Robert and Mary, born January 17, 1747
Asbury, Ann. Daughter of Hannah and George, born October 6, 1747
Asbury, Ann. Daughter of Hannah and George, died February 5, 1748
Atchison, Lucy. Daughter of Adam and Elizabeth, born December 26, 1747
Allenthrop, Sarah. Married William Price, August 5, 1748
Asberry, Ann. Married John Wilson, August 16, 1748
Asbury, William. Married Jean Aukerum, January 13, 1749
Aukerum, Jean. Married William Asbury, January 13, 1749
Ashby, Fransisina. Daughter of Winifred and Elias, born March 15, 1749
Ashby, Thomas. Son of Robert and Mary, born March 5, 1749
Anglis, William. Son of Christopher, born March 9, 1749
Adie, Martha. Wife of Hugh, died October 19, 1749
Aubury, Henry. Son of George and Hannah, born February 10, 1750
Atchison, Rosinah. Daughter of Adam and Elizabeth, born May 6, 1750

Angel, Margaret. Daughter of Samuel and Ann, born
May 29, 1750
Ashby, Jess. Son of Margaret, born May 20, 1750
Angell, John. Married Milley Harvey, October 5, 1750
Adams, John. Married Honora Carty,
September 23, 1750
Asbury, Thomas. Married Martha Jennings,
December 1, 1751
Asbury, Mary. Daughter of John and Jean, born
September 20, 1750
Adams, William. Son of John and Honora, born
April 17, 1751
Ashby, Elisha. Son of Elias and Winifred, born
December 26, 1751
Ashby, Thomas. Married Mary Maccullough,
November 14, 1751
Ashby, Millie. Daughter of Robert and Mary, born
September 11, 1751
Atchison, Jean. Daughter of Adam and Elizabeth,
born April 13, 1752
Angel, Ann. Daughter of Samuel and Ann, born
April 2, 1752
Asbee, Mary Ann. Daughter of Thomas, born
July 30, 1752
Anderson, John. Married Sarah Carney,
November 28, 1752

Angel, George. Son of John and Mildred, born
October 20, 1752
Asbury, Ann Harris. Daughter of Benjamin and Sarah,
born April 21, 1753
Asbury, Benjamin. Son of John and Jean, born
July 20, 1753
Anderson, Baily. Son of John and Sarah, born
November 13, 1753
Ashby, Wilmoth. Daughter of Robert, Jr., born
October 28, 1753
Allenthrop, Margaret. Married John Read,
March 5, 1754
Angel, Franky. Daughter of Samuel and Ann, born
February 7, 1754
Asbrook, Nancy. Daughter of Jane, born June 11, 1754
Angel, Frances. Daughter of John and Mildred, born
August 18, 1754
Adie, William. Married Elizabeth Parinder,
July 25, 1754
Asbury, Nelly. Daughter of George and Hannah, born
June 13, 1754
Asbee, Elizabeth. Wife of Robert, died
October 15, 1754
Allen, George. Departed this life December 3, 1754
Asbee, Elizabeth. Daughter of Mary and Thomas,
born November 3, 1754

Abbot, John.   Son of John, was born January 6, 1755
Asbury, William Boling.   Son of John and Jane, born
January 20, 1755
Asbury, Frances.   Wife of Benjamin, died
May 8, 1755
Asbury, Mary.   Daughter of George, died July 5, 1755
Ashby, John.   Married Sarah Maccullough,
February 26, 1756
Atchison, Nathanel.   Son of Adam and Elizabeth, born
February 1, 1756
Ashby, Catharine.   Married Isaac Murphy,
January 1, 1756
Ashby, John.   Son of John, was born June 6, 1756
Ashby, William.   Son of Robert, baptized
July 25, 1756
Anderson, Scarlet.   Son of John and Sarah, born
June 20, 1756
Abbot, Rachel.   Married Peter Knight,
December 19, 1756
Asbury, Eliza.   Daughter of Benjamin, born
December 23, 1756
Adie, Ann Fisher.   Daughter of William and Elizabeth,
born November 29, 1756
Abbot, George.   Son of John, was born May 11, 1757
Ashby, Hanknsson.   Son of Thomas and Mary, born
February 6, 1757

OVERWHARTON PARISH REGISTER. 7

Asbury, Jeremiah. Son of George and Hannah, born
June 21, 1757
Amely, Bridget. Married Thomas Riddle,
February 5, 1758
Abbott, Ann. Married Ephrine Knight,
February 12, 1758
Abbot, John. Married Margaret Lyon,
January 15, 1758
Abbot, John. Son of John, was baptized
January 6, 1758
Anderson, Lela. Was baptized April 9, 1758
Ashby, Bailey. Son of John and Sarah, born
November 22, 1858

B.

Bussel, Thomas. Son of James and Martha, born
January 27, 1727
Brent, Innis. Son of Charles and Hannah, born
July 24, 1727
Brent, Mary. Daughter of Charles and Hannah, born
May 25, 1732
Brent, Charles. Son of Charles and Hannah, born
June 11, 1735
Baker, Anne. Daughter of Edward, born April 1, 1737
Brent, Jean. Daughter of George and Catharine, born
April 10, 1738

Baker, Eleanor.   Daughter of Edward, born
                                    March 6, 1739
Brent, Susannah.   Daughter of Benjamin and Mary,
                              born November 29, 1739
Brent, Hugh.   Son of Charles and Hannah, born
                                    November 3, 1739
Bethel, William.   Married Jean Hurst,
                                    December 26, 1739
Ball, William.   Son of Edward and Sarah, born
                                    January 14, 1740
Bethel, James.   Son of Edward and Mary, born
                                    January 27, 1740
Bethel, John.   Son of Elizabeth, born January 24, 1740
Bridwell, Isaai.   Married Abigail Green,
                                    January 20, 1740
Baliwoel, Martha.   Departed this life April 13, 1740
Bridwell, Elizabeth.   Married Arron Garrison,
                                    May 10, 1740
Barret, Ellen.   Married Rev. Daniel McDonold,
                                    July 26, 1740
Bridwell, Elizabeth.   Daughter of John, died
                                    October 1, 1740
Bridwell, William.   Son of John and Lucy, born
                                    October 19, 1740
Brent, George.   Son of George and Catharine, born
                                    October 23, 1740

Byrom, Sarah. Daughter of Cuthbert and Sarah, born November 14, 1740

Baker, Jean. Daughter of Edward, born December 29, 1740, and died January 21, 1741

Bethel, James. Son of Edward, died January, 1741

Butler, Thomas. Married Mary Mason, April 7, 1741

Ball, Caleb. Son of John, died June 21, 1741

Bell, Thomas. Married Mary Latham, June 25, 1741

Brown, Frances. Daughter of Dr. Gustavus Brown, of Charles County, Maryland. Married the Rev. John Moncure, Rector of this Parish, June 18, 1741

Brooks, Matthew. Married Mary Box, August 23, 1741

Box, Mary. Married Matthew Brooks, August 23, 1741

Burton, Lettie. Married Alexander Jefferies, September 30, 1741

Burchel, Nanny. Daughter of Charles and Margaret, born October 12, 1741.

Botts, Elizabeth. Daughter of Seth and Lib, born October 3, 1741

Bethel, Peggy. Daughter of William and Jean, born November 30, 1741

Botts, Thomas. Died at Robert Ashby's, March 9, 1742

Brent, William. Son of Charles and Hannah, born
May 19, 1742
Bannester, John. Son of William, died March 20, 1742
Baker, Edward. Son of Edward and Ann, born
January 4, 1742
Barber, James. Son of John and Elizabeth, born
August 16, 1742
Brent, Captain William. Died at Aquia,
August 17, 1742
Byram, Elizabeth. Married Adam Atchison,
October 20, 1742
Berry, Lawrence. Son of Sarah, born
December 23, 1742
Bazell, William. Son of Hannah, born
January 13, 1743
Bridwell, Sarah. Daughter of John, born
January 13, 1743
Byram, John. Son of Cuthbert and Sarah, born
January 19, 1743
Baylis, John. Son of Mulrain and Winifred, born
February 19, 1743
Brooks, Matthew. Married Jean Jack, February, 1743
Bridwell, William. Son of Abraham, died
April 5, 1743
Byram, John. Son of Cuthbert and Sarah, died
March 20, 1743

Bridwell, Sarah. Daughter of Abigail, born
May 23, 1743
Boling, Edward. Married Mary Suddeth,
May 4, 1744
Bridwell, Isaac. Son of Abraham and Mary, born
June 17, 1743
Bell, John. Son of Thomas and Mary, born
July 2, 1743
Baylis, John. Son of Mulrain, died July 16, 1743
Byram, Liny. Married William Gough,
October 19, 1743
Butler, Thomas. Departed this life December 3, 1743
Barby, Joseph. Son of Thomas, baptized
March 18, 1744
Brent, Mary. Daughter of Benjamin and Mary, born
March 13, 1744
Botts, William. Son of Seth and Lib, born
April 16, 1744
Brent, George. Son of Charles and Hannah, born
June 7, 1744
Burchell, Charles. Son of Charles, born
July 10, 1744
Bethel, John. Son of Edward and Mary, born
June 23, 1744
Byram, Winifred. Daughter of Cuthbert and Sarah,
born September 26, 1744

Berry, Sarah.   Married John Ellis, September 30, 1744
Briand, Mary.   Married John Fling,
                                            December 31, 1744
Burris, William.   Son of Thomas and Mary, born
                                            December 19, 1744
Bridwell, John.   Son of Isaac and Abigail, born
                                            December 7, 1744
Bell, John.   Son of Thomas and Mary, died
                                            October 27, 1744
Bell, George.   Married Ann Hanson, April 15, 1745
Burchell, Charles.   Died at his home, March 25, 1745
Butler, Joseph.   Married Ann Carter,
                                            November 28, 1745
Butler, Margaret.   Married Alexander Nelson,
                                            February 21, 1745
Barbee, Mary.   Married William Cotney,
                                            February 24, 1745
Boalin, Jean.   Married John Asberry,
                                            February 25, 1745
Bridwell, Robert.   Married Elizabeth Jones.
                                            January 13, 1745
Baylis, Peggy.   Daughter of Mulrain, born
                                            February 2, 1745
Broderick, Sarah.   Married John Camon, July 8, 1745
Broderick, Christopher.   Married Sarah Hammet,
                                            December 19, 1744

Bridwell, Mary. Daughter of John and Lucy, born
June 19, 1745
Bassiet, Isaac. Married Mary Rhodes, May 18, 1745
Bell, Charity. Daughter of Thomas, born
October 20, 1745
Black, William. Married Ann Dent, October 17, 1745
Bethel, Mary. Married Joseph Lee,
November 14, 1745
Broderick, Mary. Daughter of Christopher and Sarah,
born October 20, 1745
Bell, Mary. Daughter of Ann, born January 7, 1746
Bridwell, Thomas. Son of Jacob and Elizabeth, born
January 21, 1746
Balls, John. Married Margaret Williams,
January 2, 1746
Burton, Priscilla. Daughter of William, born
January 17, 1746
Bridwell, Mary. Daughter of John and Lucy, died
February 22, 1746
Bannister, Henry. Son of Susannah, born
April 29, 1746
Bridwell, Mildred. Daughter of Samuel and Mary,
died March 23, 1746
Botts, Aaron. Son of Seth, born July 30, 1746
Boan, Elizabeth. Married Jacob Begoley,
August 4, 1746

Begoley, Jacob. Married Elizabeth Boan,
August 4, 1746
Burchell, Margaret. Married George Hinson,
December 29, 1746
Byram, Milley. Daughter of Elizabeth, born
December 10, 1746
Baylis, John. Died at his home, December 8, 1746
Bell, Elizabeth. Daughter of Andrew and Mary,
October 26, 1746
Begoley, William Larien. Son of Jacob and Elizabeth,
baptized November 1, 1746
Bolling, John. Son of Edmund and Mary, born
September 14, 1746
Blackman, Hannah. Married Joseph Noble,
September 7, 1746
Bridwell, William. Son of Isaac and Abigal, born
February 10, 1747
Bryan, Lucy. Daughter of Cuthbert, born
January 29, 1747
Battoo, James. Married Winney Holiday,
February 12, 1747
Battoo, Mary. Daughter of James and Winifred, born
April 29, 1747
Bussel, James. Son of Winifred, born May 20, 1747
Bethel, Mary. Daughter of Edward and Mary, born
July 23, 1747

Bridwell, Sarah. Daughter of Abraham, born
July 25, 1747
Baker, John. Married Rebecca Lunsford,
June 8, 1747
Baley, Simson. Married Elizabeth MacCarty,
December 24, 1747
Baylis, Winny. Daughter of John and Mary, born
November 1, 1747
Baylis, Mary. Married John Baylis, October 8, 1747
Baylis, John. Married Mary Baylis, October 8, 1747
Bell, Elizabeth. Daughter of George and Ann, born
January 31, 1748
Bussel, Hannah. Married John Honey,
February 2, 1748
Bettson, Thomas. Married Jane Merringham,
April 14, 1748
Byram, Millie. Daughter of William and Sarah, born
March 28, 1748
Bridwell, Margaret. Daughter of Jacob, born
January 12, 1748
Balls, John. Son of John and Margaret, born
March 20, 1748
Berry, Benjamin. Son of Richard and Sarah, born
June 10, 1748
Botts, Joseph. Son of Seth, born June 23, 1748
Bush, George. Son of George, born August 10, 1748

Bettson, Thomas. Son of Thomas and Jane, born
                                July 23, 1748
Berry, Benjamin. Was baptized August 1, 1748
Bussel, Winifred. Married Phillip Payton,
                                September 15, 1748
Bell, James William. Son of Andrew and Mary, born
                                October 14, 1748
Burn, James. Married Catharine Champ,
                                October 14, 1748
Balls, Ann. Married Samuel Hawes, February 16, 1749
Balls, Edward. Married Sarah Crosby,
                                November 24, 1749
Berry, Bridget. Married Samuel Mitchel,
                                January 30, 1749
Basnet, Abrahm. Died February 8, 1749
Bethel, Joseph. Died September 15, 1748
Bethel, Samuel. Son of William, born February 9, 1749
Bethel, Elizabeth. Daughter of Edward and Mary,
                                born May 26, 1749
Burn, Elizabeth. Was baptized April 16, 1749
Boling, Nancy. Daughter of Edmund and Ann, born
                                April 26, 1749
Bradley, Nancy. Daughter of David and Margaret,
                                born April 2, 1749
Bethel, Sith. Married Robert Hammet,
                                February 7, 1749

Bennet, Nickolas. Married Elizabeth Knight,
June 12, 1749
Barry, Thomas. Married Catharine Jones,
August 5, 1749
Bridwell, John. Son of John and Lucy, born
August 10, 1749
Bridwell, Mealy. Son of Samuel, born August, 1749
Basnett, Ann. Daughter of Isaac and Mary, born
September 3, 1749
Balls, Lydia Beek. Daughter of John and Margaret,
born October 21, 1749
Barbee, Catharine. Was born November 1, 1749
Barbee, Judy. Daughter of Thomas and Margaret,
born October 21, 1749
Bland, Moses. Married Jane Wiggonton,
January 14, 1750
Bridwell, Mealy. Son of Samuel, died
November 8, 1749
Berry, Mary. Daughter of Richard and Sarah, born
January 19, 1749
Baker, John. Son of John, born January 4, 1750
Bromley, Betty. Daughter of William and Judith,
born January 3, 1750
Barbee, Betty. Married William Smith,
January 1, 1750
Bethel, William. Died February 19, 1750

Bridwell, George. Son of Isaac and Abigal, born
January 26, 1750
Bragg, Peggy. Daughter of Joseph, born April 9, 1750
Balls, Caleb. Son of Edward and Sarah, born
April 14, 1750
Boling, Joannah. Married William Fuell,
February 17, 1750
Byram, Lizzie. Daughter of William and Sarah,
March 12, 1750
Byram, Cuthbert. Son of Cuthbert, born
January 6, 1750
Bridwell, Isaac. Son of Abraham, died May 2, 1750
Bailis, Winifred. Married Henry Robinson,
August 1, 1750
Bowman, John. Married Elizabeth Elliot,
December 23, 1750
Bridwell, Margaret. Married Henry Wiggonton,
November 12, 1750
Bridwell, Betty. Married Richard Simms,
October 15, 1750
Brent, Catharine. Wife of George, died
January 21, 1751
Betty, William. Son of Simpson, born
February 3, 1750
Bell, Jonathan. Son of George and Ann, born
January 7, 1751

OVERWHARTON PARISH REGISTER. 19

Barby, Ann. Married Garner Burges,
                            February 19, 1751
Burges, Garner. Married Ann Barby,
                            February 19, 1751
Barbee, William. Son of Thomas, born April 3, 1751
Botts, Elizabeth. Died April 17, 1751
Bailly, Thomas. Married Ann Waller, July 10, 1751
Burges, Peggy. Daughter of Garner and Ann, born
                            July 27, 1751
Botts, Joshua. Son of Seth, born July 24, 1751
Balls, Sarah. Wife of Edward, died July 24, 1751
Burn, Judith. Daughter of James, born May 24, 1751
Bayles, Betty. Daughter of John and Mary, born
                            October 20, 1751
Balls, George. Son of John, Jr., and Margaret, born
                            October 9, 1751
Bethel, Sith. Daughter of Edward and Mary, born
                            March 10, 1751
Belsher, Merriam. Married Alexander Manatear,
                            December 24, 1751
Bush, John. Son of George and Mary, born
                            December 20, 1751.
Balls, Mollie. Daughter of Henry and Isabel, born
                            December 13, 1751
Baxter, Alexander. Married Mary Byram,
                            November 28, 1751

Byram, Mary. Married Alexander Baxter,
November 28, 1751
Bouchard, William. Married Mary Stringfellow,
November 12, 1751
Brown, John. Married Hannah Cook,
November 28, 1751
Bridwell, Benjamin. Son of John, born April 15, 1752
Bragg, Phœbe. Daughter of Joseph, born
March 25, 1752
Boling, William. Son of Edmund and Mary, born
March 8, 1752
Brooks, Sarah. Married John Wilson,
February 7, 1752
Batto, Lithy. Daughter of James and Winifred, born
February 17, 1752
Bailis, Mary. Daughter of John and Mary, baptized
January 19, 1752
Berry, Sarah. Daughter of Richard and Sarah, born
January 13, 1752
Bannister, Nathan. Married Ann Eaves, May 24, 1752
Barbee, Thomas. Son of Thomas, born
October 18, 1752
Beach, James. Died at William Wright's,
December 17, 1752
Betty, Ann. Daughter of Simpson and Elizabeth,
born February 9, 1753

Bruing, William. Married Keziah Simmons,
                                February 4, 1753
Brent, Catharine. Married James Wren,
                                March 27, 1753
Bradley, Margaret. Wife of David, died
                                January 3, 1753
Burchel, William. Departed this life at George Hinson's, April 14, 1753
Byron, Sarah. Daughter of William and Sarah, born
                                May 28, 1753
Brown, Rauleigh Travers. Son of John and Hannah,
                                born July 13, 1753
Benson, Catharine. Daughter of Charles and Judith,
                                born August 29, 1753
Bell, George. Son of George and Ann, born
                                August 12, 1753
Burn, Catharine. Daughter of James and Catharine,
                                born August 3, 1753
Balls, Hezhzeba. Son of John, baptized
                                July 1, 1753
Beach, George. Married Susanna Duke,
                                December 23, 1753
Bridwell, Elizabeth. Daughter of Jacob and Elizabeth,
                                born December 26, 1753
Bridwell, Isaac. Son of Isaac and Abigal, born
                                December 9, 1753

Byram, Winifred.   Married William Routt,
                                    November 27, 1753
Burton, William.   Married Rachel Porch,
                                    October 7, 1753
Brent, Mary.   Married William Wright,
                                    October 18, 1753
Bell, George.   Son of George and Ann, baptized
                                    October 1, 1753
Bridwell, Samuel.   Drowned in Quantico Run,
                                    November 27, 1753
Burges, Mollie.   Daughter of Garner, baptized
                                    December 9, 1753
Berry, William.   Son of Richard and Sarah, born
                                    January 12, 1754
Bussel, George.   Married Catharine Randel,
                                    January 8, 1754
Bailis, Jesse.   Son of John and Mary, born
                                    February 4, 1754
Berry, William.   Married Ann Porch,
                                    February, 26, 1754
Bussel, James.   Married Martha Hill,
                                    February 24, 1754
Bethel, Edward.   Son of Edward, born
                                    April 30, 1754
Battoo, John Holliday.   Son of James, baptized
                                    May 19, 1754

Beach, Susannah. Daughter of George and Susannah,
baptized August 18, 1754
Bell, John. Son of Thomas and Mary, born
July 26, 1754
Brown, Joshua. Married Alice Lunsford,
July 21, 1754
Brent, James. Son of Charles, died
September 6, 1754
Brent, Catharine. Married James Douglass,
October 1, 1754
Bridwell, George. Son of John and Lucy, born
December 10, 1754
Bussel, Thomas. Son of James and Martha, born
November 15, 1754
Barbee, John. Son of Thomas, was born
November 12, 1754
Balls, William. Son of Henry and Isabel, born
December 14, 1754
Botts, John. Son of Sith and Lib, born
October 25, 1754
Balls, Nathanel William. Son of John, Jr., baptized
January 26, 1754
Bridwell, George. Son of John and Lucy, baptized
January 26, 1755
Burges, William. Married Bathsueba Courtney,
January 19, 1755

Bradley, David. Married Elizabeth Simmons,
April 17, 1755
Brown, John. Married Jean Noland, August 24, 1755
Burk, John. Married Elizabeth Farlow,
August 31, 1755
Bethany, Thomas. Married Mary Ann Criswell,
December 21, 1755
Bell, George. Son of George and Ann, born
September 3, 1755
Bell, Elizabeth. Was baptized September 28, 1755
Bussell, Agathy. Daughter of William, baptized
October 26, 1755
Byram, Nancy. Daughter of John, baptized
November 2, 1755
Burton, Samuel. Son of William and Rachel, born
April 20, 1756
Betty, Lottie. Daughter of Simpson and Elizabeth,
born April 11, 1756
Bridwell, Samuel. Son of Jacob and Elizabeth, born
March 6, 1756
Botts, Sarah. Married James Wiggonton,
February 9, 1756
Benson, Enoch. Married Mary Doial,
February 15, 1756
Barby, Sarah. Daughter of Thomas and Margaret,
born January 28, 1756

Brown, Cicy. Was baptized January 18, 1756
Brent, Charles. Departed this life January 13, 1756
Brent, Mary. Married Zackrias Lewis,
August 24, 1756
Bethel, Mary. Daughter of Edward, born
August 10, 1756
Bell, Thomas. Son of Thomas, born
December 24, 1756
Bolling, Elizabeth. Married Robert Mays,
December 27, 1756
Balls, Heptizitah. Son of John, Jr., died
December 17, 1756
Blueford, Jemimma. Married Robert English,
November 22, 1756
Brown, William. Married Sarah Ellen Grogg,
December 11, 1756
Brent, Susanna. Married Dr. John Southland,
September 15, 1756
Baylis, Christopher. Son of Jean, born
September 9, 1756
Bell, William. Son of James, was born
January 11, 1757
Baylis, William. Married Ann Gough,
January 19, 1757
Brooke, Hannah. Married Alexander Taylor,
February 24, 1757

Brent, Jane. Married Richard Graham,
February 10, 1757
Bussell, Anna. Daughter of James and Martha, born
April 11, 1757
Barbee, Betty. Daughter of Thomas, born
March 23, 1757
Brown, Pearson. Was baptized March 6, 1757
Bridwell, Simon. Son of John and Lucy, born
August 11, 1757
Botts, Jenny. Daughter of Seth and Lib, born
January 8, 1757
Bussel, Betty. Daughter of Hannah, born
February 7, 1756
Blackburn, Edward. Married Margaret Harrison
May 26, 1757
Bruing, Ann. Married Saxfield Noxal,
August 8, 1757
Boling, Elizabeth. Daughter of Edmund and Mary,
born October 30, 1757
Butcher, James. Son of William and Mary, born
September 10, 1757
Balls, Charles. Son of John and Margaret, born
February 13, 1758
Bussel, ———. Married Sarah Day, February 5, 1758
Byram, Peter. Married Martha Horton,
March 26, 1758

Bradley, William. Married Margaret Fortick,
March 28, 1758
Bridwell, ———. Married Lucy Lea, April 9, 1758
Barbee, Joseph. Son of Thomas and Margaret,
baptized June 28, 1758
Bush, Elizabeth. Daughter of George and Mary,
born February 20, 1758

C

Carter, John. Son of James and Mary, born
May 7, 1727
Carter, James. Son of James and Mary, born
March 31, 1729
Carter, William. Son of James and Mary, born
January 11, 1731
Carter, George. Son of James and Mary, born
March 25, 1733
Carter, Catharine. Daughter of James and Mary,
born April 1, 1735
Carpenter, Stephen. Son of John and Mary, born
June 24, 1737
Crosby, Uriel. Son of George and Sarah, born
August 19, 1738
Courtney, Anne. Married Henry Foley,
December 24, 1738
Cornish, Charles. Married Elizabeth Smith,
December 17, 1738

Chapman, Jane.   Daughter of Taylor and Margaret,
                                born January 25, 1739
Chimp, William.   Married Catharine Taylor,
                                January 31, 1739
Colson, Charles.   Married Elizabeth Norton.
                                February 1, 1739
Carpenter, John.   Son of John and Mary, born
                                May 15, 1739
Chapman, Taylor.   Married Margaret Markham,
                                September 13, 1739
Chapman, Jane.   Daughter of Taylor and Margaret,
                                born January 25, 1741
Chambers, Sarah.   Married William McDuell,
                                December 26, 1739
Cosby, James.   Son of Peter and Susannah, born
                                February 27, 1740
Cooper, Joseph.   Son of Joseph and Elizabeth, born
                                July 22, 1740
Chin, Lettie.   Daughter of Rawleigh and Elizabeth,
                                born October 17, 1740
Clutterbuck, Mary.   Daughter of William and Mary,
                                born October 25, 1740
Carter, Hugh.   Son of James and Mary,
                                born November 8, 1740
Combs, William.   Son of Mason and Sarah, born
                                November 28, 1740

Carberry, James. Son of Edward and Mary, born
                                November 17, 1740
Chapman, Jane. Daughter of Taylor, died
                                December 12, 1740
Carberry, Edward. Departed this life
                                February 24, 1741
Clark, Catherine. Died at James Suddith's, May 7, 1741
Cave, James. Son of William and Anne, born
                                April 24, 1741
Combs, Jean. Married John Ashby, May 11, 1741
Campbell, James. Married Elizabeth Milliner,
                                September 27, 1741
Crosby, Ann. Daughter of George and Sarah, born
                                October 1, 1741
Chapman, William. Son of Taylor and Margaret,
                                born September 12, 1741
Carney, Thomas. Son of John and Mary, born
                                December 18, 1741
Cockley, Robert. Married Sarah Sinclair,
                                September 21, 1740
Coffy, Frances. Daughter of Peter, died
                                January 5, 1741
Coffee, James. Son of Peter and Susannah, born*
                                February 27, 1741
Coffee, Lydia. Daughter of Peter and Susannah, born
                                January 25, 1742

Cook, Jane. Married William Pritchet,
January 26, 1742
Cassity, Catherine. Married Philip Mathews,
January 4, 1742
Cooper, Juhonias. Son of Joseph and Betty, born
February 20, 1742
Cammel, William. Married Mary Smith,
July 25, 1742
Cave, William. Died at his house, August 14, 1742
Cole, Catharine. Married Philip Prichet,
June 24, 1742
Craven, Francesana. Married Samuel Makanes,
November 14, 1742
Cave, James. Son of William and Anne, died
January 6, 1743
Cotton, John. Married Susannah Smith,
February 17, 1743
Combs, Anne. Daughter of Mason and Sarah, born
March 28, 1743
Champ, John. Son of William and Catharine, born
March 10, 1743
Corbin, William. Married Sarah Jenkins,
January 1, 1743
Champ, John. Son of William, died August 6, 1743
Carter, Charles. Son of James, born
October 10, 1743

Carter, James. An honest, good man, died.
October 24, 1743
Coffee, Benjamin. Son of Peter and Susannah, born
October 9, 1743
Cooper, John. Son of Joseph and Elizabeth, born
December 4, 1743
Carney, Traverse. Son of John and Mary, born
January 17, 1744
Carney, Daniel. Son of John and Mary, died
January 28, 1744
Crosby, George. Married Mary Huges,
January 6, 1744
Crosby, Sally. Daughter of George and Sarah, born
March 3, 1744
Cunningham, William. Son of Morris, born
March 21, 1744
Carpenter, Thomas. Son of John and Mary, born
August 7, 1744
Carter, Dale. Son of Charles and Lucy, born
August 9, 1744
Corbin, William. Married Sarah Want,
August 2, 1744
Champ, Lansdell. Daughter of William and
Catharine, born December 1, 1744
Coffey, Mary. Married James Kendal,
February 25, 1745

Carney, Absolom. Son of John and Mary, born
                                    January 27, 1745
Combs, Sarah. Daughter of Mason and Sarah, born
                                    February 25, 1745
Cotney, William. Married Mary Barbee,
                                    February 24, 1745
Cooper, Enos. Son of Joseph and Elizabeth, born
                                    April 26, 1745
Carter, John. Married Mary Butler,
                                    February 4, 1745
Carpenter, William. Son of John and Mary, born
                                    May 5, 1742
Clarnes, Ann. Married Andrew Kenney,
                                    November 30, 1744
Carter, Ann. Married Joseph Butler,
                                    November 28, 1745
Cooper, John. Married Elizabeth Pownall,
                                    March 30, 1745
Cannon, John. Married Sarah Broderick,
                                    July 8, 1745
Carr, Easter. Married Peter Reynolds, June 2, 1745
Crosby, Anne. Daughter of George and Mary, born
                                    May 30, 1745
Crosby, George. Departed this life, December 5, 1745
Chinn, Lizzie. Daughter of Betty, born
                                    October 18, 1745

Cooke, Elizabeth. Departed this life,
                                October 20, 1745
Cavenaugh, Edward. Died at Rawleigh Chinn's,
                                January 11, 1742
Crosby, Anne. Daughter of George, died
                                October 31, 1745
Crosby, Sally. Daughter of George and Mary, died
                                October 28, 1745
Cotney, John. Son of William, born
                                November 10, 1745
Corbin, Peter. Son of William and Sarah, born
                                April 23, 1745
Camp, Hannah. Daughter of Mary, born
                                March 26, 1746
Cash, Peter. Son of Peter and Charity, born
                                July 17, 1746
Carter, Joseph. Married Margaret Mason,
                                November 27, 1746
Champe, Rosomond. Daughter of William and
                Catharine, born November 18, 1746
Castello, Ann. Married Richard Sayer,
                                September 30, 1746
Carpenter, Benjamin. Son of John and Mary, born
                                October 5, 1746
Combs, Mason. Son of Mason and Sarah, born
                                February 21, 1747

Carter, Judith. Daughter of Charles and Lucy, born
March 17, 1747
Cannaday, William. Married Margaret Linee,
January, 16, 1747
Crosby, George. Son of George and Mary, born
September 1, 1747
Carney, Mary. Daughter of John and Mary, born
October 16, 1747
Cave, Elizabeth. Married Keene Withers,
December 21, 1747
Cave, Ann. Married Thomas Dent,
December 3, 1747
Connally, Dorothy. Married Robert Read,
November 10, 1747
Champ, William. Departed this life,
November 13, 1747
Carter, Mary Ann. Daughter of Joseph and Margaret,
born December 7, 1747
Corbin, John. Son of William and Sarah, born
November 22, 1747
Cannon, Ellis. Son of John and Sarah, born
January 3, 1748
Courtney, Elizabeth. Daughter of William, born
January 1, 1748
Carter, Robert. Son of Robert and Winifred, born
February 14, 1748

Chinn, Betty.   Married Solomon Waugh,
April 13, 1748
Cooper, Thomas Simmons.   Son of Joseph, born
May 29, 1748
Chinn, Rawleigh.   Married Sarah Lacy,
September 2, 1748
Carpenter, Ann.   Daughter of John and Mary, born
October 16, 1748
Champ, Catharine.   Married to James Burns,
October 14, 1748
Clarke, Lucy.   Married Stephen Pilcher,
December 7, 1748
Crosby, Sarah.   Married Edward Balls,
November 24, 1748
Carpenter, Nanny.   Daughter of John, baptized
November 27, 1748
Carty, Peter Murphy.   Son of Honour, died
December 1, 1748
Cowper, Thomas Simmons.   Son of Joseph, died
February 2, 1749
Crump, Benjamin.   Married Hannah James,
February 2, 1749
Corbin, Mary.   Daughter of William and Sarah,
baptized April 9, 1749
Chinn, Margaret.   Daughter of Rawleigh and Sarah,
born May 14, 1749

Combs, Winny. Daughter of Mason and Sarah, born
May 14, 1749
Congers, Sarah Pattison. Married Thomas Hampton,
June 1, 1749
Cash, Elizabeth. Married Calvert Porter,
September 21, 1749
Cooper, Spencer. Son of Joseph, born
October 22, 1749
Corbin, John. Married Frances Fant,
December 7, 1749
Cooke, Margaret. Married William Horton,
December 21, 1749
Carney, Jane. Daughter of John and Mary, born
December 21, 1749
Corbin, William. Was born November 10, 1749
Cartee, Honour. Delivered of a male child, which
died soon after, November 20, 1749
Chapman, Taylor. Departed this life
November 10, 1749
Cannon, John. Son of John, born February 1, 1749
Conyers, Ann Holland. Married Edward Payne,
February 27, 1750
Carter, Lucy. Daughter of Charles and Lucy, born
February 16, 1750
Cornell, John. Son of Margaret, born March 31, 1750
Crap, James. Married Joyie Hinson, June 3, 1750

Cooper, Bridget.   Married John Sylva, July 1, 1750
Cabbage, John.   Married May Jenkins,
                                July 10, 1750
Carter, Mary.   Daughter of Robert and Winifred,
                                born May 21, 1750
Cash, Elizabeth.   Was baptized June 24, 1750
Chinn, Hannah.   Married John Risen,
                                October 20, 1750
Carty, Honora.   Married John Adams,
                                September 23, 1750
Carter, Judith.   Daughter of Charles and Lucy, died
                                December 18, 1750
Corbin, William.   Son of John and Francis, born
                                February 7, 1751
Collie, James.   Married Ann Cornwall,
                                February 21, 1751
Cornwall, Ann.   Married James Collie,
                                February 21, 1751
Cash, Elizabeth.   Departed this life, March 9, 1751
Cash, Jean.   Married William Waters, April 6, 1751
Chinn, ———.   Married Mathew Gregg,
                                August 15, 1751
Carter, Lucy.   Daughter of Charles and Lucy, died
                                August 22, 1751
Cartee, Thomas.   Died at Stephen Pilcher's,
                                June 18, 1751

Carter, Solomon. Married Mary Marony,
May 26, 1751
Cannaday, Franky. Daughter of John and Rose, born
May 29, 1751
Cabbige, Elizabeth. Daughter of John and Mary,
born April 7, 1751
Cook, Hannah. Married John Brown,
November 28, 1751
Cooper, Vinient. Son of Joseph and Elizabeth, born
October 10, 1751
Combs, Wilmot. Daughter of Mason, born
October 5, 1751
Corbin, Margaret. Daughter of William and Sarah,
born January 17, 1752
Cannon, Henry. Son of John and Sarah, born
April 10, 1752
Cooper, Vinient. Son of Joseph and Elizabeth, died
March 15, 1752
Condring, Jane. Daughter of Richard, born
January 11, 1752
Conwell, Barnet. Son of Margaret, born
April 17, 1752
Carter, James. Son of John, Jr., baptized
August 30, 1752
Carter, Jedisiah. Son of Robert, was born
July 29, 1752

Carter, James. Son of John and Leana, born
                                July 17, 1752
Cocklen, Margaret. Married William Todd,
                                October 23, 1752
Carney, Sarah. Married John Anderson,
                                November 28, 1752
Carter, Margaret. Wife of Joseph, died
                                March 12, 1752
Carter, Margaret. Daughter of Joseph, born
                                March 11, 1752
Cooper, Jess. Son of Joseph and Elizabeth, born
                                April 14, 1753
Cubbige, Mary. Daughter of John, born
                                April 15, 1753
Carpenter, George. Son of John and Mary, born
                                March 24, 1753
Cannaday, Sethe. Married Edward Gill,
                                February 4, 1753
Cannaday, Ann. Daughter of John and Rosanna,
                            born March 2, 1753
Carter, Catharine. Daughter of Jeremiah, born
                                January 28, 1753
Carter, Elizabeth. Daughter of Solomon, baptized
                                January 15, 1753
Coleman, John. Son of John and Isabel, born
                                August 6, 1753

Chinn, Ann.   Daughter of Rawleigh, Jr., born
                                December 15, 1754
Crap, John.   Son of James, Jr., was born
                                October 7, 1753
Carter, Catharine.   Daughter of Charles, born
                                October 15, 1753
Cash, James.   Son of Peter and Charity, born
                                October 26, 1753
Colburn, John.   Son of John, died February 3, 1754
Carter, William.   Died at Mary Edward's,
                                September 3, 1753
Chinn, Joseph.   Departed this life, January 28, 1754
Cooke, Travers.   Married Mary Doniphan,
                                February 26, 1754
Carter, Catharine.   Daughter of James, born
                                April 21, 1754
Carter, John.   Son of John and Leanna, born
                                June 1, 1754
Carrow, Frances.   Daughter of Mary, born at Richard
                                Fistoe's, June 29, 1754
Cannon, William.   Son of John and Sarah, born
                                July 4, 1754
Cuiberford, James.   Married Elizabeth Holdbroke,
                                September 15, 1754
Carter, Margaret.   Daughter of Joseph, died
                                October 11, 1754

OVERWHARTON PARISH REGISTER. 41

Cooke, John. Died at Robert Fristoe's,
September 27, 1755
Carney, Oxesby. Son of John and Mary, born
January 2, 1755
Courtney, Bathsheba. Married William Burges,
January 19, 1755
Cooke, John. Son of Travers and Mary, born
February 5, 1755
Carter, Joseph. Married Lettie Linton,
February 5, 1755
Coleman, Lizzie Ann. Daughter of John and Isabel,
born February 12, 1755
Carter, Milly. Daughter of Robert, born
March 22, 1755
Croscuel, Ruth. Married Peter Stacey,
May 25, 1755
Cooke, Ann. Married Thomas Roach,
December 28, 1755
Carter, Anthony. Son of Joseph, born
December 14, 1755
Carter, William. Son of John and Leanna, born
November 22, 1755
Carter, Catharine. Married William Davis,
November 27, 1755
Congers, Theodosia. Married James O'Daneal,
October 19, 1755

OVERWHARTON PARISH REGISTER.

Cubbige, William, Son of John and Mary, born
September 29, 1755
Carter, Henry. Son of Jeremiah, born
September 1, 1755
Criswell, Mary Ann. Married Thomas Bethany,
December 21, 1755
Collie, Charles. Son of James and Ann, born
January 25, 1756
Carpenter, Charles. Son of John and Mary, born
September 6, 1756
Cooper, Thomas. Son of Joseph and Elizabeth, born
September 20, 1756
Corbin, James. Son of John and Frances, born
November 8, 1756
Corney, Anthony. Son of Ann and John, born
October 13, 1756
Corney, Henry. Son of John, baptized
November 25, 1756
Cummings, John. Married Lettice Phillips,
February 21, 1757
Cooke, Mott. Son of Travers and Mary, born
March 17, 1757
Cannon, Sarah. Daughter of John, born
June 9, 1757
Carter, Tabitha. Daughter of Jeremiah, born
December 11, 1757

OVERWHARTON PARISH REGISTER. 43

Crosby, Mary. Daughter of George and Mary, born
November 14, 1757
Coleman, Jesse. Son of John and Isabel, born
September 3, 1757
Cooper, William. Married Elizabeth Pliford,
January 5, 1758
Carter, Andrew. Son of Joseph, born June 16, 1758

D.

Daniel, Peter. Married Sarah Travers, July 15, 1736
Daniel, Hannah. Daughter of Peter and Sarah, born
September 9, 1737
Dillon, Anne. Married William Hacker, May 21, 1738
Davison, Andrew. Married Sarah McInteer,
November 5, 1738
Dows, Annie. Married William Miller,
March 5, 1738
Davison, James. Son of Andrew and Sarah, born
November 22, 1739
Dunaway, Mary. Daughter of Samuel and Elizabeth,
born January 6, 1740
Dunaway, Mary. Married James Stuart,
February 12, 1740
Doniphon, Alexander. Married Mary Waugh,
June 17, 1740
Dawist, Samuel. Son of Arthur, died
September 1, 1740

OVERWHARTON PARISH REGISTER.

Duffy, Stela. Daughter of Margaret, born
November 28, and died December 4, 1740

Daniel, Travers. Son of Travers and Francis, born August 4, and baptized privately,
August 5, 1768

Daniel, Travers. Son of Peter and Sarah, born
May 26, 1741

Daniel, Travers, and Frances Moncure, Jr., were married at "Claremont" October 7, 1762, by the Rev. Mr. James Scott.

Dalton, James. Son of James and Rachel, born
July 10, 1741

Davison, Andrew. Son of Andrew and Sarah, born
January 9, 1742

Dunaway, Sarah. Married James Marten,
January 22, 1741

Dent, Arthur. Married Elizabeth Manuel,
December 11, 1742

Doniphan, William. Son of Alexander and Mary,
born March 20, 1742

Duwest, Elizabeth. Married Morton Holiday,
July 28, 1742

Day, Francis. Son of Francis and Mary, born
September 29, 1742

Dillon, James. Married Margaret Warner,
November 16, 1742

OVERWHARTON PARISH REGISTER. 45

Doniphon, Anne. Married George White,
August 4, 1743
Dent, Mary. Daughter of Arthur and Elizabeth,
born November 8, 1743
Dunaway, Laton. Son of Daniel, died
January 31, 1744
Dunaway, Daniel. Married Jean Judd,
March 1, 1744
Doniphon, Elizabeth. Daughter of Alexander and
Mary, born April 18, 1744
Dawson, Jean. Married George Knight,
December 25, 1744
Dobie, Anne. Daughter of Anne, born
October 25, 1744
Davison, William. Son of Andrew and Sarah, born
October 25, 1745
Day, John. Son of Francis and Mary, born
February 8, 1745
Dickinson, Mary. Daughter of Ann and Edward
born February 15, 1745
Dunaway, Charity. Daughter of Joseph, born
March 7, 1745
Dunaway, Gothe. Daughter of Joseph and Elizabeth,
born May 22, ——
Daniel, Elizabeth Travers. Daughter of Peter and
Sarah, born May 16, 1745

Dalton, Anne. Daughter of John, baptized
September 29, 1745
Dent, Anne. Married William Black,
October 17, 1745
Duncomb, Rosamond. Married Anthony Horten,
October 27, 1745
Dent, James. Son of Arthur, born
December 21, 1745
Dinwiddie, Elizabeth. Married Gerrard Fowke,
November 26, 1745
Davids, Elizabeth. Daughter of John and Ann, born
March 2, 1745
Deckon, Margaret. Married James Reynold,
August 19, 1746
Dillon, James. Married Ann Suddeth,
July 24, 1746
Doniphon, Anne. Daughter of Alexander and Mary,
born February 28, 1747
Davis, Thomas. Son of John, born August 8, 1747
Day, Mary Ann. Daughter of Frances, born
September 28, 1747
Dent, Thomas. Married Ann Cave, December 3, 1747
Donaldson, John. Married Ann McMurry,
December 31, 1747
Dunaway, Jean. Daughter of Joseph, born
January 2, 1748

Devane, Mary. Married John Herrod,
August 21, 1748
Davis, John. Son of John, was born
November 11, 1748
Dunaway, Eton. Son of Daniel, born April 12, 1749
Dunaway, Eton. Son of Daniel, died
September 9, 1749
Dunawoy, Ezekiel. Was baptized July 23, 1749
Dawson, Christopher. Married Jane George,
February 16, 1750
Doniphan, Alexander. Son of Alexander and Mary,
born March 12, 1750
Davis, Nanny. Daughter of John, born
March 28, 1750
Dunaway, Jane. Wife of Daniel, died
October 28, 1750
Dunaway, Isaac. Son of Daniel, born
September 20, 1750
Dooling, Nancy. Daughter of Robert, born
October 31, 1750
Day, Margaret. Daughter of Francis, born
January 2, 1751
Daffin, Keziah. Daughter of Judith and Henry, born
March 30, 1751
Dooling, Margaret. Daughter of John, born
December 25, 1751

Dunaway, Daniel. Departed this life,
December 12, 1751
Dunaway, Elizabeth. Married Benjamin Lokon,
February 25, 1752
Doyson, John. Son of Christopher and Jean, boan
July 28, 1751
Dooling, Mary Ann. Daughter of Robert, born
April 5, 1753
Donophon, Mott. Son of Alexander and Mary, born
June 10, 1752
Davis, Susannah. Married Richard Smith,
November 17, 1752
Dial, Mitchel. Married Mary Smith,
November 19, 1752
Davis, Isaac. Son of John, born February 7, 1753
Dick, Moses. Son of Jane, born January 23, 1753
Duwest, Elizabeth. Daughter of Mary, born
January 6, 1753
Duke, Susanna. Married George Beach,
December 23, 1753
Dawson, Sarah. Daughter of Jean and Christopher,
born September 15, 1753
Doniphon, Mary. Married Travers Cooke,
February 26, 1754
Dowling, Nicholas. Married Elizabeth Dunaway,
June 30, 1754

Dunaway, Elizabeth. Married Nicholas Dowling,
June 30, 1754
Dunaway, Isaac. Married Mary Ann Tolson,
May 25, 1754
Dawson, Henry. Married Betty Turner,
December 15, 1754
Dooling, James. Son of Robert, born May 9, 1755
Douglass, James. Married Catharine Brent,
October 1, 1754
Dabney, George. Married Mary Waller,
September 11, 1754
Dawson, William and Henry. Sons of Jean and
Christopher, born May 27, 1755
Diskin, John. Married Frances MacCarty,
June 19, 1755
Dawson, Sarah. Daughter of Christopher, died
July 15, 1755
Dawson, William and Henry. Died June 15, 1755
Davis, William. Married Catharine Carter,
November 27, 1755
Duwest, Elizabeth. Married George Mason,
October 21, 1755
Doial, Mary. Married Enoch Benson,
February 15, 1756
Dawson, Henry. Son of Christopher, born
June 27, 1756

Driscol, Derby. Married Jean Noble, October 4, 1756
Douglass, George. Son of James and Catharine, born December 2, 1756
Dooling, Nancy. Daughter of Nicholas, died October 24, 1756
Douglass, George. Departed this life, December 17, 1756
Daniel, Hannah. Married George Hedgman, November 27, 1756
Day, Robert. Married Mary Gunn, January 16, 1757
Day, Winny. Daughter of Roberson and Mary, born October 15, 1758
Dunaway, Benjamin. Son of Isaac and Mary, born November, 27, 1757
Day, Sarah. Married —— Bussel, February 5, 1758
Darlow, Thomas. Married Margaret Lynne, April 9, 1758
Dawson, Jane. Daughter of Christopher and Jane, born March 14, 1758

E.

Edwards, Elizabeth. Married William King, May 21, 1738
Eaves, William. Son of Thomas and Catharine, born November 9, 1739
Elkin, David. Son of William and Martha, born February 14, 1742

OVERWHARTON PARISH REGISTER.   51

Edwards, Jess. Son of Ignatius and Mary, born
February 14, 1742
Elliot, Samuel. Married Easter Flood, August 9, 1742
Eaves, Thomas. Son of Thomas and Catharine, born
August 15, 1742
Eaves, Anne. The wife of Thomas, died
February 6, 1742
Edrington, Thomas. Son of William, born
August 17, 1743
Edwards, John. Son of Ignatius, died
February 24, 1744
Edwards, James. Son of Meredith and Mary, born
February 22, 1744
Eaton, Mary. Daughter of William, born
May 22, 1744
Ellis, Sith. Daughter of John and Sarah, born
July 22, 1745
Edwards, Ignatius. Had a daughter Anne, by Mary,
July 17, 1745
Edwards, James. Departed this life October 11, 1745
Edwards, Elizabeth. Daughter of Meredith and Mary,
born December 22, 1746
Eaves, Winifred. Married Peter Wigginton,
October 13, 1747
Elliot, Samuel. Married Elizabeth Wiggerson,
May 20, 1747

Eaton, Sarah. Daughter of William, baptized
September 20, 1747
Edwards, John. Son of Robert and Sarah, born
March 20, 1748
Edwards, Meredith. Son of Meredith and Mary, born
September 12, 1749
Edwards, Sarah. Daughter of Ignatius and Mary,
born June 28, 1748
Elkins, Margaret. Daughter of William, born
August 7, 1747
Elliot, Ann. Daughter of Samuel and Elizabeth, born
July 10, 1748
Elliot, Samuel. Departed this life, November 30, 1748
Edrington, Christopher. Son of William, born
April 16, 1749
Edwards, Meredith. Departed this life
October 16, 1749
Edwards, Matthews. Son of Robert and Sarah, born
August 27, 1749
Ellis, Millis. Was baptized September 30, 1750
Edwards, Ignatius. Departed this life,
October 15, 1750
Elliot, Elizabeth. Married John Bowman,
December 23, 1750
Edrington, Ann. Daughter of William, born
March 19, 1751

Edwards, Andrew. Married Betty Waugh,
                                May 7, 1751
Eaves, Thomas. Departed this life March 10, 1752
Edwards, Betty. Daughter of Andrew and Betty,
                          born February 7, 1752
Edwards, Betty. Daughter of Andrew and Betty,
                             died August 23, 1753
Edwards, Billy. Son of Andrew and Betty, born
                                October 1, 1753
Eaves, Ann. Married Nathan Bannister,
                                *May 24, 1752
Edrington, John. Son of William, born
                             November 14, 1753
Ellis, Jezreel. Son of Sarah, born August 28, 1753
Edghill, Jean. Daughter of Thomas, born
                                March 18, 1754
Edwards, Jean. Daughter of Robert and Sarah, born
                            September 29, 1754
Edzar, James. Married Eleanor Grianan,
                             November 22, 1754
Earle, Therdosian Scott. Daughter of Samuel and
                Elizabeth, born November 14, 1754
Edwards, Bridget. Married Jeremiah Spilman,
                              January 16, 1758
Edgar, Esdras. Son of James and Eleanor, born
                              February 25, 1758

Edwards, William. Married Eleanor Wheeler,
February 12, 1756
Edrington, James. Son of William and Betty, born
February 24, 1756
Edwards, Robert. Son of Robert and Sarah, born
February 6, 1756
Edwards, Nancy. Daughter of Andrew and Betty,
born March 6, 1756
Eaves, Hannah. Married John Stark, May 29, 1756
English, Rose. Daughter of John and Mary, born
May 30, 1756
Earle, Betty. Daughter of Samuel and Elizabeth,
born September 6, 1756
English, Robert. Married Jemima Blueford,
November 22, 1756
English, Sarah. Daughter of Robert and Jemima,
born January 23, 1757
Edwards, Isaker. Married Sarah Stacey, May 16, 1757
Edwards, Andrew. Married Elizabeth Withers,
January 19, 1758

F.

Fowke, William Chandler. Son of Chandler and
Mary, born September 4, 1720
Fowke, John. Son of Chandler and Mary, born
January 17, 1725

Fowke, Elizabeth. Daughter of Chandler and Mary,
    born April 27, 1727
Fowke, Chandler. The young son of Chandler and
    Mary, born September 3, 1732
Fowke, Ann. Younger daughter of Chandler and
    Mary, born September 4, 1737
Fowke, Sarah. Daughter of Chandler and Mary, born
    August 10, 1734
Fowke, Ann. Daughter of Chandler and Mary, died
    December 8, 1732
Fowke, Sarah. Daughter of Chandler and Mary, died
    October 14, 1739
Fowke, Susannah. Daughter of Chandler and Mary,
    born October 24, 1739
Frogg, John. Married Elizabeth Strother,
    November 9, 1738
Foley, Henry. Married Anne Courtney,
    December 24, 1738
Fristoe, Daniel. Son of Richard, Jr. and Grace, born
    December 7, 1739
Fowke, John. Son of Chandler and Mary, died
    April 16, 1740
French, Betty. Married James Waugh,
    August 22, 1740
Fristoe, John. Son of Richard and Grace, born
    June 6, 1741

Fowke, Richard. Son of Chandler and Mary, born
December 11, 1741
Foley, Hannah. Daughter of John and Rosina, born
April 20, 1742
Fristoe, William. Son of Richard, died
May 12, 1742
Fristoe, Richard. Son of Richard and Grace, born
July 9, 1742
Flood, Easter. Married Samuel Elliot,
August 9, 1742
Fowke, William. Departed this life,
October 24, 1742
Fletcher, George. Married Sarah Grigsby,
January 1, 1743
Fowke, William. Son of Chandler and Mary, born
May 31, 1743
Fletcher, Sarah. Daughter of Charles, born
May 31, 1743
Foley, Mary. Married Benjamin Stringfellow,
June 15, 1743
Fant, Catharine. Married Alexander Simpson,
July 17, 1743
Fowke, William. Son of Chandler and Mary, died
December 2, 1743
Fristoe, George. Son of Richard and Grace, born
April 10, 1744

Foley, John.   Married Sarah Poole,
                                December 11, 1744
Fling, John.   Married Mary Briand,
                                December 31, 1744
French, Margaret.   Married Peter Hansbrough,
                                February 26, 1745
Fowke, Captain Chandler, of Gunston Hall, in Stafford
            County.   Died February 10, 1745
Fant, George.   Son of William and Catharine, born
                                June 5, 1745
Fristoe, Jean.   Daughter of Richard and Grace, born
                                September 8, 1745
Fowke, Gerrard.   Married Elizabeth Dinwiddie,
                                November 26, 1745
Fletcher, Sarah.   Daughter of Charles, baptized
                                May 31, 1746
Fletcher, Elizabeth.   Married Benjamin Allenthrop,
                                August 19, 1746
Foster, George.   Married Margaret Grigsby,
                                December 22, 1746
Fletcher, Abraham.   Married Priscilla Grigsby,
                                November 28, 1746
Fowke, Robert Dinwiddie.   Son of Gerrard and
            Elizabeth, born September 20, 1746
Fristoe, William.   Son of Richard and Grace, born
                                March 29, 1747

Fitzhugh, Catharine. The wife of Thomas, died
　　　　　　　　　　　February 26, 1748
Fristoe, George. Son of Richard, died May 12, 1748
Fant, Margaret. Married Thomas Barbee,
　　　　　　　　　　　September 29, 1748
Fristoe, Richard. Married Mary Hayes,
　　　　　　　　　　　November 24, 1748
Fernsly, James. Married Sarah Robinson,
　　　　　　　　　　　December 3, 1748
Foregast, James. Died at William Wright's,
　　　　　　　　　　　December 15, 1748
Fristoe, George. Son of Richard and Grace, born
　　　　　　　　　　　January 8, 1749
Fant, Nathaniel. Son of William and Catharine, born
　　　　　　　　　　　January 15, 1749
Foley, Barrett. Son of John and Rosanna, born
　　　　　　　　　　　February 14, 1749
Ford, Mary. Daughter of David and Mary, born
　　　　　　　　　　　February 9, 1749
Fletcher, George. Departed this life March 16, 1749
Foster William. Married Nanny Jordan,
　　　　　　　　　　　June 15, 1749
Fant, Frances. Married John Corbin,
　　　　　　　　　　　December 7, 1740
Fuell, William. Married Johannah Boling,
　　　　　　　　　　　February 12, 1750

Fristoe, George. Son of Richard and Grace, died
  December 7, 1750
Foxworthy, Sarah. Married Daniel Green,
  October 16, 1750
Fuell, Eleanor. Daughter of William and Hannah,
  born October 9, 1750
Foster, Elizabeth. Daughter of William and Ann,
  born February 26, 1751
Ford, David. Son of David, born April 1, 1751
Fristoe, Robert. Son of Richard and Grace, born
  April 5, 1751
Fristoe, Mary. Departed this life March 26, 1751
Fristoe, Martha. Married Josuah King,
  December 12, 1751
Foxworthy, Thomas. Married Sarah Nubal,
  December 25, 1751
Fritter, Moses. Married Elizabeth Horton,
  December 1, 1751
Foxworthy, John. Married Sarah Northcut,
  September 29, 1751
Fitzpatrick, Thomas. Son of John and Mary, born
  February 26, 1752
Foxworthy, Nickolas. Married Mary Jordon,
  January 26, 1752
Fristoe, Robert. Married Ann Rhodes,
  February 23, 1752

Fitzpatrick, John. Married Mary Waters,
February 12, 1752
Floyd, Betty Ann. Daughter of James, born
June 1, 1752
Fritter, John. Son of Moses and Elizabeth, born
December 18, 1752
Foxworthy, John. Son of Mary and Thomas, born
February 2, 1753
Fernsby, Sarah. Daughter of James and Sarah,
born February 10, 1753
Foster, Isabelle. Daughter of William and Ann, born
February 16, 1753
Foxworthy, Catharine. Daughter of Nickolas and
Mary, born March 23, 1753
Foxworthy, William. Son of John and Sarah, born
April 1, 1753
Farrow, Alexander. Married Ann Obanion,
October 5, 1753
Frazer, William. Son of Mary, born at Mary
Suddeth's, November 8, 1754
Fritter, Hugh Horton. Son of Moses and Elizabeth,
born January 6, 1754
Furguson, Elizabeth. Daughter of John, baptized
May 19, 1754
Flitter, John. Married Bridget Riggins,
March 16, 1755

French, Rachel. Daughter of Hugh, died
January 16, 1755
Farlow, Elizabeth. Married John Burch,
August 31, 1755
Flitter, Moses. Son of Moses and Elizabeth, born
October 1, 1756
Fitzhugh, John. Was baptized February 29, 1756
Fitzhugh, Susanna. Daughter of John, was baptized
February, 25, 1756
Foxworthy, Saky. Daughter of John and Sarah, born
February 1, 1756
Frazer, Mary. Daughter of Isabella, born
June 12, 1756
Furguson, Kate. Daughter of John, baptized
October 17, 1756
Fristoe, Richard. Married Virginia Waters,
February 28, 1757
Fletcher, Moses. Married Sarah Martin,
July 10, 1757
Flitter, William. Son of Moses and Elizabeth, born
October 30, 1757
Fortick, Margaret. Married William Bradley,
March 26, 1758
Foxworthy, Thomas. Son of John, born
May 12, 1758

G.

Grant, Peter. Son of John and Margaret, born November 18, 1739

Green, Abigail. Married Isaac Bridwell, January 20, 1740

Gallahan, Eleanor. Daughter of John and Penelope, born April 1, 1740

George, Elizabeth. Daughter of William and Eleanor, born May 10, 1740

Garrison, John. Son of John and Nancy, born May 17, 1740

Garrison, Arron. Married Elizabeth Bridwell, May 10, 1740

Gregg, James. Son of Matthew and Catharine, born May 18, 1740

Gregg, Elizabeth. Daughter of William, died at William Bethel's, May 15, 1740

Garrison, Mary Anne. Daughter of Arron and Elizabeth, born September 22, 1741

George, Elmore. Son of William, died November 25, 1740

George, Nickolas. Married Margaret Whitson, December 25, 1740

Green, Martha. Daughter of John and Abigail, born April 15, 1741

Gallahan, Thomas. Son of John and Eleanor, born
March 21, 1741
Goleman, Sarah. Daughter of Francis and Winifred,
born September 20, 1741
Griffin, Elizabeth. Married James Philips,
September 27, 1741
Gallahan, Elizabeth. Daughter of Solomon and
Mildred, born October 9, 1741
George, Nickolas. Son of Nickolas and Margaret,
born November 21, 1741
Grant, William. Son of John and Lydia, born
March 9, 1742
Garner, Parish. Married Margaret Sturdy,
January 2, 1742
Garret, Betty. Daughter of Robert and Mary Anne,
born May 29, 1742
Garrison, Susannah. Daughter of John and Anne,
born May 21, 1742
George, Elmore. Son of William and Eleanor, born
May 14, 1742
Goodwin, Jean. Married Henry Nelson,
October 18, 1742
Garrison, George. Son of Arron, born
November 14, 1742
Garner, James. Son of Parish and Margaret, born
November 25, 1742

Gallahan, William. Son of Solomon, born
April 26, 1743
Grigsby, Sarah. Married George Fletcher,
January 1, 1743
Gough, Glady E. Child of Thomas and Sarah, born
February 4, 1743
George, Sith. Daughter of Benjamin and Mary, born
June 30, 1743
Gallahan, John. Son of John and Eleanor,
July 9, 1743
Green, William. Married Ann Robinson,
December 18, 1743
Gough, William. Married Liny Byram,
October 19, 1743
Gough, Joshua. Son of William and Lucy, born
March 31, 1744
Grigsby, Alice. Married Benjamin Bush,
April 1, 1744
Garner, Thomas. Son of Parish, born
August 25, 1744
Green, Sarah. Daughter of Anne and William, born
September 24, 1744
Grigsby, William. Son of John and Ann, born
October 30, 1744
Grady, William. Son of William and Anne, born
November 11, 1744

OVERWHARTON PARISH REGISTER. 65

Green, George. Married Elizabeth Whitson,
December 23, 1744
Garrison, William. Son of Mary, born
December 11, 1744
George, Nanny. Daughter of Nicholas and Margaret,
born December 3, 1744
Gregg, John. Son of Matthew and Catharine, born
December 19, 1744
Garrison, John. Son of Aaron, born January 1, 1745
Garret, Constance. Daughter of Robert and Mary,
April 3, 1745
Gowing, Isabel. Wife of Peter, died March 11, 1745
Gallahan, Malerson. Daughter of Solomon, born
May 2, 1745
Gowing, Peter and Mary Sullivant. Married
May 28, 1745
Grimes, Mary. Daughter of Richard and Elizabeth,
August 26, 1745
Griffin, Thomas. Married Sarah Suddeth,
July 18, 1745
Garret, Daniel. Married Mary Holliday,
September 4, 1745
George, William. Married Mary Whitson,
November 1, 1745
Garrison, Mary. Married John Kelly,
November 1, 1745

Green, Thomas. Son of George and Elizabeth, born
November 27, 1745
Grant, Jane. Married John Glendering,
January 30, 1746
Glendering, John. Married Jane Grant,
January 30, 1746
Green, Patty. Married Wiiliam Harding,
Jnauary 20, 1746
Gallahan, Solomon. Son of Mary and Solomon, born
March 26, 1747
Green, Elizabeth. Married Richard Young,
December 27, 1746
Grigsby, Priscilla. Married Abraham Fletcher,
November 28, 1746
Grigsby, Margaret. Married George Foster,
December 22, 1746
Green, Dorcas. Daughter of William and Anne, born
December 30, 1746
Garrison, William. Son of Ann, born
October 23, 1746
Griffith, Daniel. Son of Thomas and Sarah, born
September 2, 1746
Godfrey, William. Married Rebecca Robinson,
October 26, 1746
George, John. Son of William and Mary, born
March 1, 1747

Grant, Elizabeth. Daughter of John and Lydia, born
July 28, 1747
Gough, Sarah. Married William Bryan, May 14, 1747
Green, James. Married Lucy Martin, October 4, 1748
Grigsby, Susannah. Daughter of John and Ann, born
October 10, 1747
Garret, Bryan. Son of Robert and Mary, born
November 28, 1747
Grigsby, Lettie. Married Joshua Owens,
November 10, 1747
George, Elizabeth. Daughter of Nickolas and
Margaret, born December 1, 1747
Green, James. Son of John, Jr., born
January 22, 1748
Green, George. Son of George and Elizabeth, born
February 23, 1748
Garrison, Sukey. Daughter of Aaron and Elizabeth,
born March 26, 1748
Groves, Edward. Married Mary Hearne,
September 15, 1748
Garret, Bryan. Son of Robert, died
December 18, 1748
Gallahan, Alice. Daughter of John, born
December 15, 1748
Gill, Spencer. Son of Elizabeth, died
November 3, 1748

Gill, Elizabeth. Married Joseph White,
January 31, 1749
Grace, Ellender. Daughter of Mary, born
February 7, 1749
Groves, William. Married Barbara Webster,
February 2, 1749
Green, Annas. Daughter of William and Ann, born
March 18, 1749
George, Lydia. Daughter of William and Mary, born
April 4, 1749
Gough, Sarah. Daughter of William, born
August 15, 1749
Green, Lizzie, the wife of James, died October 29, 1749
Green, George. Son of Lizzie and James, born
October 21, 1749
Garrison, Aaron. Son of Aaron, born October 1, 1749
Gallahan, Mary. Daughter of Solomon and Mary,
born January 1, 1750
Glass, Elizabeth. Married John Lindcey.
January 15, 1750
Green, Sarah. Daughter of John, born
January 20, 1750
George, Jane. Married Christopher Dawson,
February 16, 1750
Grant, Ann. Daughter of John and Lydia, born
April 8, 1750

OVERWHARTON PARISH REGISTER. 69

Godfrey, Jane. Daughter of William, and Rebecca,
born February 5, 1750
Grigsby, Rachel. Daughter of John and Ann, born
August 17, 1750
Green, Sarah. Daughter of John, died August 17, 1750
Green, Daniel. Married Sarah Foxworthy,
October 16, 1750
Grinstead, Lydia. Daughter of Peter, born
January 20, 1751
Grace, Sarah. Daughter Mary, born January 8, 1751
Grey, William. Son of Ann, born January 26, 1751
Garrison, Winny. Daughter of Aaron and Elizabeth,
born April 28, 1751
Garret, Sarah. Daughter of Robert and Mary Ann,
born March 4, 1751
George, Willmouth. Daughter of Nickolas and
Margaret, born March 4, 1751
Gorman, Mary. Married James Stanard, June 20, 1751
Green, Jess. Son of John, Jr., and Jean, born
August 20, 1751
Green, Mary. Daughter of William, born
July 21, 1751
Grey, Richard. Son of John and Margaret, born
May 15, 1751
Gregg, Mathew. Married —— Chinn,
August 15, 1751

Gain, Lizzie. Married James Matheny,
December 12, 1751
Green, Mary. Married William More,
November 28, 1751
George, Franky. Daughter of William and Mary,
born November 7, 1751
Grant, Jane. Daughter of John and Lydia, born
April 17, 1752
Gough, Nanny. Daughter of William, born
January 29, 1752
Grant, Mary. Wife of Jasper, died, and her child also,
February 27, 1752
Godfrey, James. Son of William, born July 26, 1752
Gallahan, Charles. Son of Solomon, born
May 20, 1752
Gregg, Mathew. Son of Mathew, was baptized
September 17, 1752
Garrison, Sarah. Daughter of Aaron and Elizabeth,
born April 24, 1753
Garret, Winifred. Daughter of Robert and Mary,
born March 21, 1753
Gill, Edward. Married Lethe Canaday
February 4, 1753
Grigsby, Moses. Married Mary Matheney,
August 26, 1753
Grigsby, Sarah. Married William Rose, June 5, 1753

Green, Nanny. Daughter of John, born
July 19, 1753
Going, Peter. Died at Priscilla Hayes',
May 22, 1753
Gunn, John. Married Martha Shamlin,
September 30, 1753
Green, Jacl. Daughter of William, born
November 12, 1753
Grace, John. Son of Mary, born November 4, 1753
Gaines, Frances. Daughter of Humphry and Sarah,
born November 14, 1753
George, Sarah Ann. Daughter of William, born
April 1, 1754
Green, Lizzie. Daughter of Daniel and Sarah, born
April 1, 1754
Gill, John. Married Elizabeth Williams,
March 3, 1754
Gerrard, Mary Ann. Daughter of William, baptized
February 17, 1754
Gerrard, Gerard. Son of Mary, born at John Waters',
March 14, 1755
Gashings, Isaac. Son of Sarah, born July 29, 1754
Grant, Mary. Daughter of John and Lydia, born
September 15, 1754
George, Sarah. Daughter of Nickolas and Margaret,
born October 11, 1754

Godfrey, Elizabeth. Daughter of William and
                           Rebecca, born October 28, 1754
Gallahan, Margaret. Daughter of Solomon, born
                                    October 8, 1754
Grianan, Eleanor. Married James Edzar,
                                  November 22, 1754
Gough, William. Son of William, born
                                  February 17, 1755
Green, John. Son of John, Jr., was born
                                     April 4, 1755
Garrison, Moses. Son of Aaron and Elizabeth, born
                                    March 9, 1755
Gaines, Henry. Son of Humphry and Sarah, born
                                    April 11, 1755
Goolding, Susanna. A bastard child, born
                                    March 4, 1755
Gallahan, John. Had a daughter named Mary, born
                                  February 4, 1755
Gill, Elsy. Daughter of John and Elizabeth, born
                                  January 28, 1755
Gwinn, James. Married Elizabeth Maccaboy,
                                   October 5, 1755
Green, Willliam. Son of William and Ann, born
                                    April 28, 1756
Griffin, Phillis. Died at James Hardwicks',
                                     April 9, 1756

Graves, Sarah. Married George Jeffries,
February 8, 1756
Goldsmith, John. Married Martha Powell,
January 19, 1756
Grigsby, John. Son of Moses, born
January 18, 1756
Green, Mary. Daughter of Daniel and Sarah, born
August 25, 1756
Green, John. Married Phillis Smith,
December 19, 1756
Grogg, Sarah. Married William Brown,
December 11, 1756
Green, Robert. Married Helen Lowry,
November 23, 1756
Green, Sarah. Married Snowdall Laytham,
November 25, 1756
Garner, John. Son of Samuel and Isabel, born
November 13, 1756
George, William. Son of William, born
December 1, 1756
Gerrard, Anthony. Son of Jacob, baptized
October 12, 1756
Grant, John. Son of John and Lydia, born
March 11, 1756
Graham, Richard. Married Jane Brent,
February 10, 1757

74   OVERWHARTON PARISH REGISTER.

Gallahan, Nelly. Daughter of John, born
                                February 19, 1757
Gunn, Mary.   Married Robert Day, January 16, 1757
Green, William. Son of John, born January 18, 1757
Gough, Ann. Married William Baylis,
                                January 19, 1757
Gough, Peggy. Was baptized December 23, 1757
Gerrard, Sarah. Daughter of Mary, born
                                January 15, 1757
Gaines, Sarah. Daughter of Humphrey, born
                                February 25, 1757
George, Lydia. Daughter of Nickolas and Margaret,
                                born May 29, 1757
Grigsby, Jane. Married William Rose,
                                March 14, 1758
Garrison, Milly. Daughter of Aaron and Elizabeth,
                                born June 27, 1758
Greenless, Bethsheba. Married ———, May 7, 1758
George, William. Son of William, died June 3, 1758
Green, William. Married Judith Harrel,
                                January 21, 1742

H.

Hyden, Lucy. Daughter of William and Mary, born
                                December 28, 1731
Hedgman, William. Son of Peter and Margaret,
                                born July 1, 1732

OVERWHARTON PARISH REGISTER.

Hyden, Samuel. Son of William and Mary, born
                                June 19, 1733
Hedgman, George. Son of Peter and Margaret, born
                                December 11, 1734
Hyden, Henry. Son of William and Mary, born
                                December 2, 1735
Hyden, Charity. Daughter of William and Mary,
                                born June 19, 1737
Harding, William. Son of Charles and Rachel, born
                                March 12, 1738
Hacker, William. Married Anne Dillon,
                                May 21, 1738
Hamilton, Anne. Married John Alridge,
                                June 11, 1738
Harvie, Anne. Married Richard Wine, July 23, 1738
Humphrieys, John, Jr. Married Margaret Young,
                                September 23, 1738
Hays, Catharine. Married Thomas Waters,
                                September 28, 1738
Hammet, Margaret. Daughter of William and Mary,
                                born February 10, 1739
Hyden, Richard. Son of William and Mary, born
                                March 8, 1739
Helms, Mary. Married Gabriel Muffet, July 25, 1739
Higgerson, Hannah. Married James Whealy,
                                July 8, 1739

Howard, John. Son of James and Margaret, born
September 2, 1739
Hacker, William. Son of William, born
December 9, 1739
Hurst Jean. Married William Bethel,
December 26, 1739
Harding, Anne. Daughter of Charles and Rachel,
born February 3, 1740
Horton, Townshend. Son of Snowdal and Sarah,
born April 21, 1740
Heffernon. Jane. Married Alexander Payton,
May 20, 1740
Heffernut, Sarah. Married William Wilkison,
August 21, 1740
Hyden, William. Son of William and Mary, born
September 1, 1740
Hankins, Diana. Daughter of Daniel and Hannah,
born December 8, 1740
Hurst, James. Son of Thomas and Mary, born
November 13, 1740
Harper, Sarah. Daughter of Mary and Michael,
born April 24, 1741
Hornbuckel, Franklin. Son of Richard, born
April 11, 1741
Harding Wilmouth. Daughter of Henry and
Wilmouth, born April 14, 1741

OVERWHARTON PARISH REGISTER. 77

Hurst, Landen. Son of Mary, born July 25, 1741
Heaflon, Simon. Son of William, born
October 1, 1741
Heffernon, William. Married Sarah Martin,
September 29, 1741
Hedgman, John. Son of Peter and Margaret,
born October 13, 1741
Heffernon, John. Son of James, born
November 23, 1741
Hammet, Charles. Son of William and Elizabeth,
born February 4, 1742
Harrel, Judith. Married William Green,
January 21, 1742
Higgins, John Bayham. Son of Jane, born
May 28, 1742
Holiday, Whorton. Married Elizabeth Dunest,
July 28, 1742
Harding, Jane. Daughter of Charles and Rachel,
born November 9, 1742
Hinson, Edmund. Died November 18, 1742
Hacker, John. Son of William and Anne, born
January 2, 1743
Hankins, Margaret. Daughter of Daniel and
Elizabeth, born February 6, 1743
Hickerson, John. Departed this life
February 2, 1743

Harding, Franky. Daughter of George and Jinny,
             born March 7, 1743
Hyter, William. Married Anne Hewis,
             April 3, 1743
Hewis, Anne. Married William Hyter, April 3, 1743
Higerson, Sarah Elwood. Daughter of Thomas and
             Sarah, born March 27, 1743
Heath, Milian. Daughter of Thomas and Elizabeth,
             born January 10, 1743
Hefferton, Mary Byford. Daughter of William, born
             ———, 1743
Hyden, Daniel. Son of William and Mary, born
             April 6, 1743
Hill, John. Departed this life March 19, 1743
Horton, Hoasin. Daughter of Snowdal and Sarah,
             born May 16, 1743
Higgerson, Elizabeth. Married John Waters,
             June 5, 1743
Harding, Nickolas. Son of Henry and Wilmouth,
             born July 6, 1743
Hinston, Isabel. Married James Felton,
             November 13, 1743
Homes, Henry. Died at Anthony Murray's,
             November 16, 1743
Huges, Mary. Married George Crosby,
             January 6, 1744

OVERWHARTON PARISH REGISTER. 79

Hayter, James. Son of William and Anne, born
January 32, 1744
Hammet, Mary. Daughter of William and Elizabeth,
born February 4, 1744
Hansbrough, Peter. Son of James and Lettie, born
June 12, 1744
Hyden, Daniel. Son of William, died June 5, 1744
Hughs, James. Married Agnes MacCartee,
May 6, 1744
Hurst, Nathaniel. Son of Mary, born June 6, 1744
Holdbrook, William. Married Elizabeth King,
December 8, 1744
Hammet, Sarah. Married Christopher Roderich,
December 19, 1744
Harper, Thomas. Son of Michael and Mary, born
December 31, 1744
Hogg, John. Married Eleanor Savage,
December 19, 1744
Head, Mary. Departed this life, May 21, 1745
Hanson, Ann. Married George Bell, April 15, 1745
Hayter, Anne. Wife of William, died
March 26, 1745
Harding, Charles. Son of Charles and Rachel, born
April 6, 1745
Hose, Catharine. Married Thomas Monroe,
April 16, 1745

Hansbrough, Peter. Married Margaret French,
February 26, 1745
Hughs, William. Son of Agnes and James, born
February 14, 1745
Hyden, Jacob. Son of William and Mary, born
August 18, 1745
Hornbuckle, Ann. Married Samuel Angell,
August 14, 1745
Hurst, Priscilla. Daughter of Thomas and Mary, born
June 21, 1745
Harding, William. Married Patty Green,
January 28, 1746
Horton, Venus. Daughter of Snowdel and Sarah,
born July 14, 1745
Hill, William. Married Catharine Stacey,
September 17, 1745
Head, Charles. Son of Mary, was born
May 13, 1745
Holliday, Mary. Married Daniel Garret,
September 4, 1745
Hyden, William. Son of William and Mary, died
October 21, 1745
Harvey, Elizabeth. Married Thomas Johnson,
October 19, 1745
Horton, Anthony. Married Rosamond Duncomb,
October 27, 1745

Harrison, Captain William. Departed this life,
December 1, 1745
Hart, John. Married Rachel Oran,
March 23, 1746
Holliday, Mary. Daughter of Wharton, born
April 29, 1746
Hawkins, Sarah. Daughter of Daniel, born
January 13, 1746
Hinson, George. Married Margaret Burchell,
December 29, 1746
Hansbrough, James. Son of James, born
November 11, 1746
Hansbrough, James. Son of James and Lettie, died
December 14, 1746
Harding, Winny. Daughter of George and Jean, born
December 1, 1746
Hunter, Elizabeth. Married John Kenny,
October 12, 1746
Harding, Hall. Son of William and Patty, born
October 25, 1746
Holliday, Winny. Married James Battoo,
February 12, 1747
Head, Joseph. Son of Robert and Dorothy, born
October 27, 1746
Horton, Reuben. Son of Anthony and Rosamond
born April 27, 1747

Harper, Mary. Daughter of Michael and Mary, born
February 9, 1747
Hinson, Mary. Died at John Honey's,
March 16, 1747
Hughs, Agnes. Departed this life, March 4, 1747
Higgerson, Elizabeth. Married Samuel Elliot,
May 20, 1747
Hornbuckle, Richard. Departed this life,
July 29, 1747
Horton, Francis. Daughter of Elizabeth, born
June 21, 1747
Harrison, Thomas. Married Ann Peyton,
July 2, 1747
Harding, John Scott. Son of Charles and Rachel,
born August 3, 1747
Hansbrough, William. Son of Peter, born
August 4, 1747
Hurst, John. Died the sixth day of December, 1747
Hornbuckle, Elizabeth. Married John Smith,
December 31, 1747
Holliday, John. Son of Wharton and Elizabeth, born
January 11, 1747
Horton, George. A bastard of Mary Horton, born
January 26, 1748
Honey, John. Married Hannah Bussel,
February 2, 1748

Husk, Hanny. Daughter of Thomas and Mary, born January 24, 1748
Hansbrough, Elizabeth Magdalene. Daughter of Lillie and James, born February 22, 1748
Herrod, John. Married Mary Devane, August 21, 1748
Hearne, Mary. Married Edward Groves, September 15, 1748
Hayes, Mary. Married Richard Fristoe, December 24, 1748
Hinson, Mary. Married Henry Threlkeld, November 2, 1748
Hurst, Mary. Married Owen Wingfield, November 26, 1748
Hammet, Robert. Married Lythe Bethel, February 7, 1749
Hawes, Samuel. Married Mary Ann Bails, February 16, 1749
Harding, Ann. Daughter of George and Jane, born May 29, 1749
Horton, Aden. Son of Anthony and Rosamond, born June 4, 1749
Hampton, Thomas. Married Sarah Pattison alais Congers, January 1, 1749
Harding, Thomas. Son of Charles and Rachel, born August 11, 1749

Horton, William. Married Margaret Cooke,
December 21, 1749
Herrod, William. Son of John, born
December 13, 1749
Hore, Elias. Son of Elias and Mary, born
December 31, 1749
Holliday, Keziah. Married Robert Million,
December 14, 1749
Hyden, Nathaniel. Was born December 1, 1749
Horton, John. Son of Sarah and John, born
December 23, 1749
Harper, Margaret. Was baptized December 3, 1749
Haffermon, James. Son of James, born
September 20, 1749
Hammet, William. Son of Robert and Sith, born
November 14, 1749
Hunter, John. Died at Captain Wm. Mountjoy's,
September 29, 1749
Hornbuckle, George. Died at John Smith's
September 10, 1749
Hurst, Henry. Married Ann Pyke, March 20, 1750
Hinson, Charles. Departed this life,
February 22, 1750
Hinson, Joyie. Married James Crap, June 3, 1750
Hinson, Lettie. Daughter of George, born
May 21, 1750

Harod, Margaret. Daughter of Mary, Surnamed
Deveene, February 6, 1750
Hurst, Absolum. Son of Thomas, born
May 15, 1750
Horton, Benjamin. Son of Martha, born
August 26, 1750
Hansbrough, Milly. Daughter of James, born
May 5, 1750
Harrison, Susannah. Married Robert Slaughter,
December 11, 1750
Hardwick, Haswel. Married Mary Northcut,
December 8, 1750
Harvey, Milly. Married John Angell,
October 5, 1750
Horton, Thomas. Son of Mary, born January 4, 1750
Hurst, James. Married Rosannah Jones,
April 21, 1751
Hurst, Nancy. Daughter of Henry, born
April 20, 1751
Horton, Mary. Daughter of William, born
March 22, 1751
Howard, Grace. Departed this life, February 7, 1751
Hope, Samuel. Died at Alexander Nelson's,
April 24, 1751
Howard, William. Married Elizabeth Stacey,
May 29, 1751

Horton, Elizabeth. Married Moses Fritter,
December 1, 1751
Hall, Mary. Married Charles Wawal,
November 16, 1751
Hose, Betty. Daughter of Elias and Mary, born
October 6, 1751
Hill, John. Son of William and Catharine, born
October 11, 1751
Hyden, Mary. Married John Nicholson,
April 23, 1752
Horton, Anthony. Died at the house of Hugh
Horton's, September 21, 1751
Harper, Phobe. Daughter of Michael and Mary, born
March 13, 1752
Harding, Moses. Son of Charles and Rachel, born
March 19, 1752
Hazel, Fanny. Daughter of P. Hazel, born
January 18, 1752
Hurst, Elizabeth. Daughter of James and Rosamond,
born January 10, 1752
Howard, Elizabeth. Daughter of William and
Elizabeth, born August 14, 1752
Honey, William. Son of John, baptized
July 19, 1752
Holliday, Mary. Daughter of Wharton, born
June 9, 1752

Hansbrough, Peter. Married Lydia Smith,
May 27, 1752
Hinson, Margaret. Wife of George, died
November 22, 1752
Hinson, Mary. Daughter of George and Margaret,
born October 28, 1752
Hansbrough, Gabriel. Son of James, born
November 17, 1752
Horton, Phobe. Daughter of John and Sarah, born
March 14, 1752
Hinson, Elizabeth. Daughter of Sarah, born
May 31, 1753
Hyden, Daniel. Born at his home, March 17, 1753
Hardwick, Ann. Daughter of Hasel and Mary, born
January, 4, 1752
Horton, Dunnel. Son of William and Margaret, born
January 4, 1753
Hinson, George. Married Sarah Sullivan,
February 4, 1753
Harding, Henry. Son of George and Jane, born
August 29, 1753
Hill, William. Son of William, born August 4, 1753
Hill, Martha. Daughter of James and Lydia, born
May 5, 1753
Hansbrough, Smith. Son of Peter and Lydia, born
June 30, 1753

Hughes, Elizabeth. Daughter of Ralph, born
June 30, 1753
Hurst, Henry. Son of James and Rosanna, born
December 3, 1753
Hardwick, William. Son of Hasel and Mary, born
September 5, 1753
Hughes, Doffus. Died at Mary Suddeth's,
September 14, 1753
Hill, Martha. Married James Bussel, February 24, 1754
Hedgman, Margaret. Wife of Peter, died
January 16, 1754
Holdbrook, Elizabeth. Married Samuel Earle,
January 13, 1754
Horton, Winifred. Daughter of Martha, born
July 28, 1754
Harding, George. Son of Charles and Rachel, born
July 31, 1754
Hinson, Elizah. Son of George and Sarah, born
May 27, 1754
Horton, Orpan. Daughter of John and Sarah, born
February 14, 1754
Hamilton, Henry. Was baptized February 24, 1754
Haynie, Winifred. Daughter of Charles and Elizabeth,
born February 12, 1754
Holdbrook, Elizabeth. Married James Cinberford,
September 15, 1754

Harding, Ann. Departed this life,
September 13, 1754
Hutt, Aggy. Married William Ticer,
December 15, 1754
Holliday, Jannie. Daughter of Wharton, born
September 22, 1754
Hill, George. Son of William and Catharine, born
February 19, 1755
Heath, Susanna Thomson. Married John Richards,
March 6, 1755
Humphreys, Franky. Daughter of William and Sarah,
born March 8, 1755
Horton, Snowdal. Departed this life,
January 19, 1755
Higgison, Thomas. Died at John Water's
February 21, 1755
Heckeney, Dianah. Departed this life,
January 25, 1755
Hammet, William. Married Rosamond Smith,
May 6, 1755
Horton, Phobe. Daughter of John, died
July 17, 1755
Horton, Orpha. Daughter of John and Sarah, died
August 8, 1755
Howard, Elizabeth. Wife of William, died
July 12, 1755

Honey, John. Son of John and Hannah, born
July 31, 1755
Hainsford, Stephen. Married Margaret MacCarthy,
October 14, 1755
Hainsbrough, James. Son of James, born
October 30, 1755
Hardwick, Elizabeth Daughter of Hasel and Mary,
born September 8, 1755
Hayes, Priscilla. Daughter of Thomas, baptized
November 28, 1755
Hinson, Sarah. Daughter of Lazarus and Sarah, born
November 21, 1755
Hay, Priscilla. Daughter of Thomas and Frances,
born November 8, 1755
Hore, Nathaniel Brown. Son of Elias, born
December 18, 1755
Hyden, William. Was born January 28, 1756
Hamilton, Leanna. Daughter of Henry, born
February 2, 1756
Howard, William. Married Martha Wheeler,
April 25, 1756
Hansbrough, Sarah. Daughter of Lydia and Peter,
born March 13, 1756
Harding, Ann. Married Mark Waters, July 20, 1756
Hunt, Milly. Daughter of James and Rosanna, born
August 26, 1756

Hughes, John. Son of Ralph, born
December 24, 1756
Harrison, Sarah. Married John Monroe,
September 23, 1756
Hore, Samuel Brown. Son of Elias, baptized
February 8, 1756
Hedgman, George. Married Hannah Daniel,
November 27, 1756
Horton, Beverly. Son of William and Margaret, born
April 8, 1757
Hall, Lettie. Daughter of John, born March 2, 1757
Harrison, Margaret. Married Edward Blackburn,
May 26, 1757
Holliday, Betty. Daughter of Wharton, born
June 27, 1757
Hay, Catharine. Daughter of Thomas and Frances,
born October 12, 1757
Horton, Clara. Daughter of John and Sarah, born
December 5, 1757
Hurst, James. Son of Thomas and Mary, born
March 19, 1757
Harding, Sarah. Daughter of Jean and George, born
March 26, 1758
Horton, Martha. Married Peter Byram,
March 23, 1758
Hord, Mary. Married ———, 1758

Helms, Sarah. Daughter of Samuel, born
May 25, 1758
Halley, William. Married Catharine Jeffries,
February 9, 1758
Hansbrough, Anna Violet. Daughter of James, born
April 24, 1758
Hurst, Elijah. Son of John, born February 16, 1758
Hammond, Charles. Son of John and Elizabeth, born
April 20, 1758
Higgerson, John. Married Jean Jackson,
January 20, 1741-2

I.

Isaac, Margaret. Married Alexander Suitor,
July 21, 1754
Innis, James. Son of John and Mary, born
March 11, 1752
Innis, James. Was baptized April 12, 1752
Innis, William. Son of John and Mary, born
July 9, 1757

J.

Johnston, Benoin. Son of William and Frances, born
February 4, 1740
Judd, Mary. The daughter of ———, died
May 23, 1740

Johnston, Silent. Married John Simpson,
August 17, 1740
Jackson, Sarah. Daughter of John and Sarah, born
November 2, 1740
Jackson, Jean. Married John Higgerson,
January 20, 1741-2
Jones, George. Son of John and Mary, born
March 3, 1741
Jeffries, Alexander. Married Lettie Burton,
September 30, 1741
Jackson, Henry. Son of William and Grace, born
October 8, 1741
Jones, Elizabeth Warner. Daughter of Briviton and
Lettie, born October 7, 1741
Johnston, Wilmouth. Daughter of William and
Frances, born May 17, 1742
Jeffries, Alexander. Had a child named ———, born
September 6, 1742
Jones, John. Son of John and Mary, born
October 10, 1742
James, Margaret. Daughter of George, baptized
November 21, 1742
Jenkins, Sarah. Married William Corbin,
January 1, 1743
Jack, Jean. Married Matthew Brooks,
February —, 1743

Jeffries, Silent. Married Rose Suthard,
January 19, 1744
Jones, Sarah. Married William Matheney,
March 22, 1743–4
Judd, Jean. Married Daniel Dunaway, March 1, 1744
Jackson, Sith. Was born March 23, 1744
Jones, Robert. Son of Breveton and Lettie, born
June 29, 1754
Jeffries, James. Son of Alexander, born
November 25, 1744
Jones, Elizabeth. Married Robert Bridwell,
January 13, 1745
Johnson, Thomas. Married Elizabeth Harvey,
October 19, 1745
Jones, Thomas. Married Frances Leftridge,
(Leftwich,) December 16, 1746
Jeffries, James. Married Sarah Matthews,
December 23, 1746
James, Joseph. Son of George and Mary, born
December 8, 1746
Jones, James. Married Frances Mason,
January 8, 1747
Jeffries, Susannah. Daughter of James and Elizabeth,
born April 8, 1747
Jeffries, Betty. Daughter of James and Sarah, born
August 11, 1747

OVERWHARTON PARISH REGISTER.

Jeffries, Betty. Departed this life, August 17, 1747
Jones, Eliza. Son of Thomas and Frances, born
September 22, 1747
Jones, Rose. Married John Robertson,
October 15, 1747
Jordan, Willoughby. Son of William and Sarah, born
May 8, 1748
Jeffries, Catharine. Daughter of James, born
October 25, 1747
James, Daniel. Son of George, born
December 6, 1748
James, Margaret. Daughter of George, died
October 30, 1748
James, William. Departed this life November 2, 1748
James, Hannah. Married Benjamin Crump,
February 2, 1749
Jackson, William. Departed this life, March 16, 1749
Jackson, Dianna. Daughter of William and Jane,
born May 9, 1749
Jordon, Nanny. Married William Foster,
June 15, 1749
Jones, Catharine. Married Thomas Barry,
August 5, 1749
Jackson, John. Son of Grace, born April —, 1750
Jenkins, Mary. Married John Cubbage, July 10, 1750
Johnston, Archibald. Was baptized October 21, 1750

Jones, Rosannah. Married James Hurst,
April 21, 1751
Jones, Charles. Married Elizabeth Sinclair,
April 21, 1751
Jennings, Martha. Married Thomas Asbury,
December 1, 1751
Jeffries, Elizabeth. Married Nelson Kelly,
November 4, 1751, by Mr. Macdonal
Johnston, William. Died at John Prim's
December 25, 1751
Jordan, Mary. Married Nicholas Foxworthy,
January 26, 1752
Jones, John. Married Margaret Jenkins,
November 26, 1752
Jenkins, Margaret. Married John Jones,
November 26, 1752
Johnson, Elizabeth. Departed this life,
November 13, 1752
Jones, Phillis. Married William Sturdy,
December 17, 1752
Johnson, Rachel. Was born October 23, 1752
Jackson, John. Son of Grace, died March 15, 1753
Jeffries, Lydia. Daughter of James and Sarah, born
September 17, 1754
Jackson, Grace. Died at John Peyton's,
September 17, 1754

OVERWHARTON PARISH REGISTER.

Jeffries, Joseph. Married Margaret Smith,
October 24, 1754
Johns, Jane. Daughter of Elizabeth, born
March 16, 1755
Jack, Mary. Married Simon Robinson,
August 3, 1755
Jeffries, Sarah. Daughter of Joseph and Margaret,
born August 22, 1755
Jones, Mary. Daughter of John, born
October 4, 1755
Johnson, Eleanor. Daughter of William and Tabitha,
born December 8, 1755
Jeffries, George. Married Sarah Graves,
February 8, 1756
Jeffries, Sarah. Daughter of James, baptized
April 25, 1756
Jeffries, Catharine. Married William Halley,
February 9, 1758

K.

King, William. Married Elizabeth Edward,
May 21, 1738
King, John. Son of William and Elizabeth, born
December 1, 1740
Kenton, Mary, Daughter of Mark and Mary, born
August 9, 1740

Kendal, Jesse. Son of William, Jr., born
November 4, 1740
Kirke, John. Married Sarah Robinson, June 23, 1741
Kirke, Winifred. Daughter of John and Sarah, born
April 21, 1742
Kinny, Richard. Son of James, born April 9, 1742
Kendal, Thomas. Son of William and Jemima, born
March 27, 1742
Kemp, John. Son of James and Elizabeth, born
August 28, 1742
Kirke, John Hardy. Son of Sarah, born
March 30, 1743
Kirke, Sarah. The wife of William, died
December 28, 1743
Knight, Nelly. Daughter of Leanod and Nelly, born
August 7, 1743
Kenny, William. Son of James and Ann, born
December 22, 1743
Kendal, George. Son of William and Jemima, born
January 13, 1744
Knight, Mary Ann. Daughter of Christopher, born
June 14, 1744
King, Elizabeth. Married William Holdbrook,
December 8, 1744
Kenny, Andrew. Married Ann Clarnes,
November 30, 1744

Knight, John. Married Charity Latimore,
October 23, 1750
Kendal, Jesse. Departed this life, November 18, 1740
Kirke, Randale. Son of the said John and Sarah,
born April 21, 1742
Kirk, William. Son of Sarah, born June 6, 1742
Kirke, Winifred. The daughter of John and Sarah,
born April 21, 1742
Knight, George. Married Jean Dawson,
December 25, 1744
Kirke, John. Son of John and Sarah, born
January 20, 1745
King, William. Son of William and Elizabeth, born
February 22, 1745
Kendal, James. Married Mary Coffey,
February 25, 1745
Kenny, Nancy. Daughter of Andrew and Anne, born
October 15, 1745
Kendal, Anne. Daughter of William and Jemima,
born December 6, 1745
Kenny, Thomas. Son of James and Anne, born
August 2, 1745
Kelly, John. Married Mary Garrison,
November 1, 1745
Knight, Elizabeth. Daughter of George and Jean,
born March 4, 1745–6

Knight, William. Son of Elizabeth, born
February 28, 1745–6
Kenny, John. Married Elizabeth Hunter,
October 12, 1746
King, Weathers. Son of William, died
August 20, 1747
Kirke, Elijah. Son of John and Sarah, born
July 2, 1747
Kendal, Jesse. Son of James and Mary, born
June 19, 1747
Kenny, Calib. Son of John and Mary, born
May 21, 1747
Kelly, Honour. Died at William Wright's,
August 13, 1747
Knight, John. Son of George, born October 22, 1747
Knight, William. Departed this life
November 27, 1747
Kirke, Elijah. Son of John, died November 25, 1747
Kitchen, Richard. Son of James and Mary, born
January 18, 1748
Kendal, John. Son of William and Jemima, born
March 21, 1748
Kendall, William. Married Jemimah Kirk,
May 10, 1748
Kirk, Jemimah. Married William Kendall,
May 10, 1748

Kendal, George. Married Margaret Kelly,
June 5, 1748
Kelly, Margaret. Married George Kendal,
June 5, 1748
Kendal, Joshua. Married Catharine Smith,
April 4, 1749
Kendall, John. Son of James and Mary, born
February 26, 1749
Knight, Elizabeth. Married Nicholas Bennet,
June 12, 1749
Kenny, Sarah. Daughter of James and Ann, born
April 15, 1749
Kenny, Elizabeth. Daughter of Andrew and Ann,
born August 30, 1749
Kendal, William and Samuel. Sons of William and
Jemimah, born August 30, 1749
Kendall, Jess. Son of James, died April 17, 1750
Kendall, Henry. Was baptized March 4, 1750
Kitchen, Merryman. Son of James, born
March 26, 1750
King, Nimrod. Son of William, born
November 29, 1750
Kelly, Sarah. Married William Sebastian,
June 11, 1751
Kirke, Laricha. Daughter of John and Sarah, born
May 8, 1751

Kendal, Jess. Son of Joshua, born August 21, 1751
Knight, Samuel. Son of John and Charity, born
                                August 15, 1751
King, Josiah. Married Martha Fristoe,
                                December 12, 1751
Kelly, Nelson. Married Elizabeth Jeffries,
                                November 14, 1751
Kenny, Reuben. Son of James and Ann, born
                                October 12, 1751
Kendal, John. Married Catharine Kees,
                                January 9, 1752
Kees, Catharine. Married John Kendal,
                                January 9, 1752
King, Martha. Married Joseph MacCollough,
                                February 9, 1752
Kendrick, James. Son of Patrick and Jane, born
                                January 10, 1752
Kitchen, Elizabeth. Daughter of James and Mary,
                                born January 15, 1748
Kendal, Mary Ann. Daughter of William and
                                Jemima, born April 9, 1752
Kendon, Edward. Married Mary Waller,
                                April 15, 1753
Kirke, William. Departed this life March 21, 1753
Kendal, Samuel. Son of John and Catharine, born
                                January 1, 1753

Kendal, Joshua. Son of Joshua and Catharine, born
May 27, 1753
Kirke, Sarah. Daughter of John and Sarah, born
September 5, 1753
Knight, Sarah Ann. Daughter of George and Jean,
born October 2, 1753
Kendal, Lizzie. Daughter of William and Jemima,
born April 1, 1754
Knight, Ephraim. Son of Isaac, born
February 3, 1754
Kite, John. Son of John, was baptized, July 14, 1754
Kendal, Charles. Son of John and Catharine, born
September 7, 1754
Kendrick, Isabel. Daughter of Patrick and Jane, born
October 13, 1754
Kenny, Mary Ann. Was born January 9, 1755
Kirke, Elizabeth. Daughter of John, born
November 24, 1755
Kendal, Bailey. Son of James and Mary, born
October 8, 1755
King, Elizabeth. Daughter of William, baptized
September 7, 1755
Kendal, Nancy. Daughter of Joshua and Catharine,
born December 19, 1755
Kennedy, Jane. Daughter of Milly, born
March 29, 1756

104 OVERWHARTON PARISH REGISTER.

Kennedy, Isabel. Married William Patten,
December 19, 1756
Kirk, Henry. Married Sarah Lunsford,
May 23, 1756
Knight, Peter. Married Rachel Abbot,
December 19, 1756
Kirk, Suky. Daughter of Henry and Sarah, born
April 25, 1757
King, John Edwards. Son of William, born
December 21, 1757
Knight, Christopher. Son of Peter and Rachel, born
November 7, 1757
Knight, Ephram. Married Ann Abbot,
born February 12, 1758
Kendal, Elizabeth. Daughter of John and Catharine,
born February 11, 1758
Kendal, Betty. Daughter of Joshua and Catharine,
born February 22, 1758
Kendal, Jeremiah. Son of William and Jemima, born
February 6, 1758

L.

Lewis, Walter Morgan. Married Mary Abram,
August 27, 1738
Limbrick, Susannah. Daughter of William, born
October 12, 1739

Lamb, Mary. Married Edward Malphus,
                    December 25, 1740
Linton, Mary. Married John Remy, April 6, 1740
Lowry, Judith. Daughter of William and Tabitha,
                    born February 13, 1742
Lunsford, Sarah. Daughter of William and Mary,
                    born March 7, 1744
Luns, Letty. Daughter of Bebina, born June 21, 1744
Latimore, Mary. Married Lewis Pritchet,
                    March 4, 1744
Lunsford, Hannah. Daughter of William and
                    Dinah, born June 5, 1744
Limbrick, James. Son of William and Catharine,
                    born May 10, 1744
Lawless, Thomas. Son of Mary, born
                    January 28, 1744
Lawless, Thomas. Son of Mary, died
                    September 10, 1744
Lowry, George. Son of William and Tabitha, born
                    November 24, 1744
Latham, Mary. Married Henry Suddeth,
                    June 25, 1745
Lee, Joseph. Married Mary Bethel,
                    November 14, 1745
Latham, Jane, Died at Mary Richard's,
                    January 7, 1745-6

Leftridge, Frances. Married Thomas Jones,
December 16, 1746
Lunsford, Charlotte. Daughter of William and
Dinah, born December 26, 1746
Latham, Frances. Departed this life, October 2, 1746
Latham, John. Departed this life, October 1, 1746
Lunsford, Mary. Daughter of William, born
September 7, 1746
Lowry, Tabitha. Married Jeremiah Stark,
January 29, 1747
Lunsford, Rebecca. Married John Baker,
June 8, 1747
Linee, Margaret. Married William Cannaday,
January 16, 1747
Lemmon, John. Married Eleanor McCarty,
April 10, 1748
Lymm, Joseph. Son of Rose, born March 24, 1748
Limon, James. Son of John, born August 15, 1748
Limbrich, Rachel. Married Thomas Porch,
July 22, 1748
Lacy, Sarah. Married Rawleigh Chinn,
September 2, 1748
Lunsford, Benjamin. Son of William, born
February 10, 1749
Limbrick, Vinson. Son of William, died
April 28, 1749

Lincey, John. Married Elizabeth Glass,
January 15, 1750
Lunsford, Judith. Married John Petter,
February 27, 1750
Lymm, Frank. Son of Rose, was born
April 21, 1751
Latimore, Charity. Married John Knight,
October 23, 1750
Lunsford, Hannah. Daughter of William, born
October 16, 1751
Latham, Sarah. Married William Mays,
February 9, 1752
Lemaster, Elizabeth. Daughter of Thomas and
Lettie, born January 14, 1753
Lunsford, Rowley. Married Joanna Sturdy,
June 16, 1754
Lunsford, Alice. Married Joshua Brown,
July 21, 1754
Lynah, Margaret. Daughter of Rose, born at
Peter Ront's, July 23, 1754
Linton, Lettie. Married Joseph Carter,
February 5, 1755
Lunsford, Jane. Daughter of Moses and Rachel,
born April 24, 1756
Lunsford Lettie. Married William Simpson,
January 18, 1756

Lunsford, John. Married Margaret Martyn,
January 6, 1756
Lunsford, Sarah. Married Henry Kirk,
May 23, 1756
Lewis, Zackias. Married Mary Brent,
August 24, 1756
Lowry, Helen. Married Robert Green,
November 23, 1756
Laytham, Snowdall. Married Sarah Green,
November 28, 1756
Laytham, Jemima. Daughter of Snowdall and Sarah,
born November 7, 1758
Lea, Lucy. Married ——— Bridwell,
April 9, 1758
Lunsford, Susanna. Married John Peyton,
March 28, 1758
Lane, James. Married Mary Quill,
January 12, 1758
Lunsford, Enoch. Son of John, born
born February 28, 1758
Lane, James Hardage. Married Mary Smith,
January 12, 1758
Lyon, Margaret. Married John Abbot,
January 15, 1758
Lynns, Margaret. Married Thomas Darlow,
April 9, 1758

M.

Mercer, Mason. Son of John and Catharine, born
             July 2 and died July 23, 1720
Mercer, John. Son of John and Catharine, born
             December 17, 1727
Murray, John. Son of John and Mary, born
             March 1, 1729
Mercer, Elizabeth Mason. Daughter of John and
             Catharine, born February 16, 1730
Mercer, Elizabeth Mason. Daughter of John and
             Catharine, died August 31, 1732
Mercer, John. Son of John and Catharine, died
             September 12, 1730
Mercer, George. Son of John and Catharine, born
             July 2, 1733
Mercer, John Fenton. Son of John and Catharine,
             born August 31, 1735
Mercer, James. Son of John and Catharine, born
             February 26, 1736–7
Mountjoy, Edward. Son of William and Phillis, his
             wife, born January 1, 1736
Mountjoy, William. Son of William and Phillis, born
             Sepember 28, 1737
Mercer, Sarah Ann Mason. Daughter of John and
             Catharine, born June 21, 1738

110   *OVERWHARTON PARISH REGISTER.*

Mcinteer, Sarah.   Married Andrew Davison,
                                    November 5, 1738
Murray, Sarah.   Daughter of Anthony, born
                                    February 24, 1739
Miller, William.   Married Anne Dono,
                                    March 5, 1738–9
Mathews, Elizabeth.   Married Timothy Oneal,
                                    April 22, 1739
Muffet, Gabriel.   Married Mary Helms,
                                    July 25, 1739
Markham, Margaret.   Married Taylor Chapman,
                                    September 13, 1739
McDuell, William.   Married Sarah Chambers,
                                    December 26, 1739
Miller, Anne.   Daughter of William and Ann, born
                                    December 23, 1739
Manzey, John.   Son of Peter and Elizabeth, born
                                    December 17, 1739
Matheny, Mary.   Married Edward Ponton,
                                    November 20, 1739
McDaniel, Mary.   Daughter of James and Martha,
                                    born January 6, 1740
McInteer, Joyie.   Married William Patten,
                                    January 27, 1740
Manzey, Jemima.   Daughter of John and Hester, born
                                    March 26, 1740

Masters, Mary. Daughter of Jared and Anne, born
May 4, 1740
Moyon, Rosamond. Married Stephen Phips,
June 1, 1740
Mercer, Mary. Daughter of John and Catharine, born
August 23, 1740
McDonald, Rev. Daniel. Married Ellen Barret,
July 28, 1740
McDuell, John. Son of William and Sarah, born
June 22, 1740
Mousley, James. Died at Major Peter Hedgman's
June 8, 1740
Mason, Anne. Daughter of Willam and Mary, died
August 20, 1740
Miller, Simon. Married Isabella Miller,
October 2, 1740
Miller, Isabella. Married Simon Miller,
October 2, 1740
Murray, James. Son of Anthony and Mary, died
September 26, 1740
Murphy, John. Son of Gabriel and Mary, born
September 6, 1740
Murray; Anthony. Son of Anthony and Mary, died
October 4, 1740
Malphus, Edward. Married Mary Lamb,
December 28, 1740

Million, William. Son of Robert, died
                                December 5, 1740
More, Elizabeth. Daughter of Jonathan and Elizabeth,
                                born December 20, 1740
Murray, Sarah. Daughter of Anthony and Mary, died
                                November 17, 1740
Morris, Anne. Daughter of Anne and John, born
                                November 14, 1740
Million, Elizabeth. Daughter of Robert, died
                                December 7, 1740
Monk, Robert. Departed this life, January 31, 1741
Merriman. Mary. Daughter of Adrian or Adam and
                                Elizabeth, born January 19, 1741
Martin, Francis. Son of Francis and Betty, born
                                February, 25, 1741
Montjoy, Jonathan. Son of Thomas and Elizabeth,
                                born February 28, 1741
Morris, Margaret. Daughter of Griffen and Elizabeth,
                                born February 10, 1741
Moncure. The Rev. Mr. John Moncure of this Parish
    was married to Miss Frances Brown, oldest
    daughter of Dr. Gustavus Brown, of Charles
    County, Maryland, June 18, 1741
Mason, Mary. Married Thomas Butler, April 7, 1741
Mallaken, Mary. Married Joseph Williams,
                                February 9, 1741

OVERWHARTON PARISH REGISTER. 113

Million, Anne. Daughter of Robert and Grace, died
April 8, 1741
McCarty, John. Son of William and Agnes, born,
March 27, 1741
McCarty, James. Son of John, born April 1, 1741
Milliner, Elizabeth. Married James Campbell,
September 27, 1741
Marten, Sarah. Married William Heffermon,
September 29, 1741
Mountjoy, Thomas. Son of William and Phillis,
born October 24, 1740
Mason, Lewis. Son of William, born
October 28, 1741
Murray, John. Son of Anthony, born
October 9, 1741
Mountjoy, John. Son of William and Phillis, born
October 25, 1741
Murphy, Mary. Died at Edward Malphus',
October 1, 1741
McGuirk, John. Married Rachel Wade,
December 23, 1741
Matthews, Philip Married Catharine Cossity,
January 4, 1742
Murray, Anthony. Departed this life, October 4, 1740
Mercer, Thomson Mason. Son of John and Catharine,
born April 9, 1740

Mathews, Catharine. Daughter of Samuel and Anne, born March 5, 1742

Murphy, Matthew. Son of John and Elizabeth, born August 17, 1742

Montgomery, Sarah. Wife of John, died August 30, 1742

Marten, James. Married Sarah Dunaway, January 22, 1741

Minor, Nicholas. Son of James, was born June 4, 1742

Martin, Jean. Daughter of Thomas and Sarah, born June 6, 1742

McDuell, Mary. Daughter of William and Sarah, born May 4, 1742

Monk, Priscilla. Daughter of Elizabeth, born May 7, 1742

Makanes, Samuel. Married Fransisme Cravens, November 14, 1742

Mannel, Elizabeth. Married Arthur Dent, December 11, 1742

McColin, Mary. Daughter of John, born December 30, 1742

Minor, Allender. Daughter of John and Margaret, born January 10, 1742

McDonald, William. Son of Martha and James, born January 25, 1742

Morris, John. Son of Griffen and Elizabeth, born
January 22, 1742
Malphus, Mary. Departed this life a few days after
her husband on the 19th of October, ——
Malphus, Edward. Departed this life,
September 15, 1743
Mitchel, Elizabeth. Daughter of Jedidiah, born
September 18, 1743
Murray, Nancy. Daughter of Anthony, born
October 8, 1743
Manzey, Priscilla. Married William Rassan,
October 27, 1743
Mountjoy, Mary. Daughter of William and Phillis
born November 6, 1743
McCarty, William. Departed this life,
September 15, 1743
More, Nathaniel. Married Elee Nickolas,
December 31, 1743
Montgomery, John. Married Mary Smith,
January 16, 1744
Molton, George. Married Margaret Strother,
April 6, 1744
Martin, Charles. Son of Francis and Elizabeth, born
April 22, 1744
MacFarlane, Priscilla. Daughter of Daniel, born
April 10, 1744

OVERWHARTON PARISH REGISTER.

Matheny, William.   Married Sarah Jones,
March 22, 1744

More, John.   Son of Nathaniel, born
August 1, 1744

Monk, Elizabeth.   Married William Walker,
May 23, 1744

Moncure, Frances. The wife of the Rev. John Moncure, was delivered of a son about 20 minutes after ten at night, and was privately baptized by the Rev. James Scott about two hours after by the name of John, and departed this life next morning about six of the clock, in the year 1744, and the month July 13

Moncure, Frances. The wife of the Rev. John Moncure, was delivered of a daughter about 35 minutes after 4 o'clock in the afternoon the 17th day of October, 1748, and baptized December 2d by the Rev. James Scott, who, with George Mason, Esq., were God Fathers; Miss Mary Mason and Elizabeth Brown, her God Mothers, and called Ann (see July, 1741)

MacCartee, Agnes.   Married James Hughs,
May 6, 1744

Moncure, Frances. Wife of the Rev. John Moncure,

was delivered of a son about half an hour after four in the morning, January 7, 1746–7, and baptized John, March 3, 1747, by the Rev. Mr. John Phipps; John Mercer and George Macon, Esq., his God Fathers, and Elizabeth Brown, his Aunt, his God Mother

Moncure, Frances. The wife of the Rev. John Moncure, was delivered of a daughter about fifty minutes past ten in the forenoon, September 20, 1745, and baptized Frances by the Rev. James Scott, September 28, 1745. He and George Mason (Gents.), her God Fathers; Mrs. Anne Carter, the wife of Charles Carter, Esq., and Mrs. Sarah Scott, her God Mothers

Mathews, John. Son of William, Jr., aged six years, died November 11, 1744

Manzey, Henry. Married Ann Withers, November 11, 1744

MacCoy, Elizabeth. Daughter of Murdy and Ann, born September 29, 1744

More, Mary. An orphan, died at John Water's, November 10, 1744

Monroe, Thomas. Married Catharine Hore, April 16, 1745

Morris, William. Son of Griffin and Elizabeth, born
June 20, 1745
Massey, Thomas. Married Eleanor Perender,
June 26, 1745
Moore, Nathaniel. Married Sarah Page,
September 11, 1745
Million, Winifred. Married Elias Ashby,
September 4, 1745
Mason, Lewis. Son of William, died
October 29, 1745
Morris, Mary. Married John Smith,
December 26, 1745
Manzey, Elizabeth. Daughter of Peter, born
December 20, 1745
Murray, Lettie. Daughter of Anthony and Mary,
born December 23, 1745
Moore, Sarah. Daughter of Nathaniel and Sarah,
born November 6, 1745
Matthis, Richard. Married Mary Plummer,
October 5, 1745
Million, Charky. Daughter of Robert, baptized
December 15, 1745
Matheny, Daniel, had two of his family to die,
November 4 and 24, 1745
Moussby, Anne. Died at William Mason's,
November 3, 1745

OVERWHARTON PARISH REGISTER.   119

Montjoy, Alvin. Son of William and Phillis, was
baptized February 9, 1746
Mitchel, John. Son of Jedidiah and Lydia, was
baptized April 6, 1746
Moss, Prisby. Son of Sylvester and Elizabeth, born
May 24, 1746
Montgomery, Jane. Daughter of John, born
August 20, 1746
Mathews, Sarah. Married James Jeffries,
December 23, 1746
Mason, Margaret. Married Joseph Carter,
November 27, 1746
Mason, Elizabeth. Departed this life,
November 5, 1746
Mason, Frances. Married James Jones,
January 8, 1747
Monroe, George Hore. Son of Thomas and Catharine,
born September 3, 1747
Mason, John. Married Mary Nelson,
November 27, 1747
McConchie, William. Married Bridget Whitecotton,
November 10, 1747
Million, William Bennet. Son of Robert and Grace,
born December 23, 1747
MacMurry, Ann. Married John Donaldson,
December 31, 1747

MacCarthy, Elizabeth. Married Simson Bailey,
December 24, 1747
MacMachon, Byron. Married Jane Moore,
December 30, 1747
Moore, Jane. Married Byron MacMachon,
December 30, 1747
Macaboy, Mortbrough. Married Elizabeth Pumphrey,
December 27, 1747
More, Mary. Daughter of Nathaniel and Sarah, born
Jnauary 31, 1748
Million, William Bennet. Baptized
September 22, 1748
Merringham, Jane. Married Thomas Bettson,
April 14, 1748
McCarty, Eleanor. Married John Summon,
April 10, 1748
Mitchell, Barnaby Le Gosh. Son of Jedidiah and
Lydia, born March 10, 1748
Murray, Phobe. Daughter ot Anthony, born
April 1, 1748
Manzy, Peter. Son of Peter and Elizabeth, born
May 19, 1738
McConchie, Richard. Son of William, born
July 10, 1748
Minor, Susannah. Daughter of William, born
August 22, 1748

Moncure, Ann. Daughter of Rev. John Moncure and
Frances, his wife, born October 17, 1748
Moring, James. Died at Capt. William Mountjoy's,
September 23, 1748
Mountjoy, George. Son of William and Phillis, born
September 9, 1748
Martin, Lacy. Married James Green, October 4, 1748
Mason, William. Son of John and Mary, born
November 30, 1748
Murphy, Peter. Was baptized November 8, 1748
Monroe, Thomas. Was baptized November 2, 1748
Mitchel, Samuel. Married Bridget Berry,
January 30, 1749
Montgomery, John. Son of John, born
April 3, 1749
Minor, Amelia. Daughter of John, born July 7, 1749
Morris, James. Died at John Smith's,
August 28, 1749
Million, Robert. Married Heziah Holliday,
December 14, 1749
McCoy, Alexander. Son of Mundy and John, born
October 20, 1749
Million, John. Son of Robert, died October 1, 1749
Montgomery, John. Son of John, died
October 22, 1749
Macaboy, Murthough. Died January 1, 1750

Macaboy, Murthough. Son of Murthough and
Elizabeth, born January 19, 1750
Moss, Meredith. Son of Silvester and Elizabeth, born
January 4, 1750
Mitchell, William. Son of Samuel and Bridget, born
January 27, 1750
Matheny, Mary. Departed this life, January 12, 1750
More, Sarah. Daughter of Sarah and Nathaniel, born
April 26, 1750
More, Sarah. Died at William George's plantation,
March 5, 1750
Matheny, Job. Son of William and Ann, born
February 6, 1750
Millian, Benjamin. Son of Robert, born July 5, 1750
Macconchie, Bridget. Married Stephen Pilcher,
December 1, 1750
Montgomery, Robert. Son of John and Mary, born
November 13, 1750
Murray, Margaret. Married John Ogiboy,
October 7, 1750
Murray, Anthony. Departed this life at his own
home, October 5, 1750
Mings, James. Married Susannah Pattison,
September 7, 1750
Mathews, George. Married ——— Chinn,
August 15, 1750

OVERWHARTON PARISH REGISTER.   123

Murdock, John. Married Margaret Strother,
                                October 26, 1750
Million, Jemima. Daughter of Robert, born
                                November 13, 1750
Mobley, Elizabeth. Died at Henry Robinson's,
                                September 4, 1750
Minor, John, Sr. Died at his home,
                                January 12, 1750-1
Mason, John. Son of John and Mary, born
                                February 18, 1750
Morris, Young. Son of Griffin, born March 25, 1751
Mason, Mary Thomas. Married Samuel Selden,
                                April 11, 1751
Mathews, Mary. Married John Waller, July 4, 1751
Marony, Mary. Married Solomon Carter,
                                May 26, 1751
Montjoy, Elizabeth. Daughter of William and
                        Phillis, born May 26, 1751
Matheny, James. Married Lizzie Gain,
                                December 12, 1751
MacCollough, Benjamin. Married Elizabeth Whitson,
                                December 19, 1751
MacCothough, Hannah. Married Benjamin Tolson,
                                December 31, 1751
Manatear, Alexander. Married Merriam Belsher,
                                December 24, 1751

Maccullough, Mary.   Married Thomas Ashby,
                                November 14, 1751
More, William.   Married Mary Green,
                                November 28, 1751
Monroe, Isabel.   Daughter of Thomas and Catharine,
                                born November 12, 1751
Monslow, John.   Died at the house of John Water's,
                                October 3, 1751
McDaniel, Margaret.   Daughter of Jane and James,
                                born January 8, 1752
Mitchel, Elizabeth.   Daughter of Samuel and Bridget,
                                born January 19, 1752
Mays, James.   Son of Joseph, was born
                                February 1, 1752
MacDaniel, Margaret.   Married John Powell,
                                February 10, 1752
Manzy, Elizabeth.   Married Peter Murphy,
                                February 9, 1752
Murphy, Peter.   Married Elizabeth Manzy,
                                February 9, 1752
MacCollough, Joseph.   Married Martha King,
                                February 9, 1752
Mays, William.   Married Sarah Laythium,
                                February 9, 1752
Montgomery, Elizabeth.   Daughter of John and
                                Mary, born April 20, 1752

OVERWHARTON PARISH REGISTER.

Mathews, Jean. Daughter of John, born
June 23, 1752
Moss, Triplet. Son of Sylvester and Elizabeth, born
August 9, 1752
Mills, Elizabeth. Married Edward West,
October 6, 1752
McCoy, William. Son of Mudy and Ann, born
October 15, 1752
More, John. Son of Nathaniel and Sarah, born
September 20, 1752
Murphy, Eleanor. Daughter of Peter and Elizabeth,
baptized October 29, 1752
Macinteer, William. Son of Alexander, born
November 7, 1752
Mays, George. Son of William and Sarah, born
February 7, 1753
Mason, Daniel. Married Elizabeth Nelson,
January 30, 1753
Matheny, Mary. Daughter of James and Elizabeth,
born January 16, 1753
Moore, Isaac. Son of William and Mary, born
March 25, 1753
Matheny, Mary. Daughter of William and Ann,
born April 2, 1753
Matheny, Mary. Married Moses Grisby,
August 26, 1753

Moncure, Jean.   Daughter of the Rev. John Moncure,
                        born May 22, 1753
Matheny, William.   Son of Thomas and Hannah,
                        born July 26, 1753
Mason, Nelson.   Son of John and Mary, born
                        August 6, 1753
Million, Sithy.   Daughter of Robert of Keziah, born
                        April 2, 1753
Montjoy, Margaret.   Daughter of William and Phillis,
                        born April 2, 1753
Mills, Margaret.   Married James Sconkraft,
                        October 14, 1753
Mays, George.   Son of William, died
                        November 14, 1753
Mays, Lydia.   Daughter of Joseph and Sarah, born
                        February 25, 1754
Montgomery, John.   Son of John and Mary, born
                        January 26, 1754
Manzeys, George.   Departed this life at John
                        Manzey's, January 10, 1754
Macculough, William.   Son of Benjamin and
                        Elizabeth, born May 19, 1754
Macinteer, Gabriel.   Son of Alexander, born
                        May 24, 1754
More, Ann.   Daughter of Nathaniel and Sarah, born
                        June 8, 1754

Mays, Jeany. Daughter of William and Sarah, born
October 15, 1754
More, William. Son of William and Mary, born
December 30, 1754
Murphy, Ann. Daughter of Peter and Elizabeth,
born February 14, 1755
Montjoy, Margaret. Daughter of Capt. William
Montjoy, died March 1, 1755
Matheny, Ann. Daughter of Ann and William, born
March 18, 1755
Morris, Anthony. Son of Griffin and Elizabeth, born
January 28, 1755
McCarty, Ignatius. Departed this life at his home,
February 18, 1755
McCarty, Frances. Married John Diskin,
June 19, 1755
Macquatty, David. Married Mary Skaines,
May 6, 1755
Macquatty, Nancy. Daughter of David and Mary,
born July 10, 1755
Maccoy, Elizabeth. Daughter of Murdy, died
June 5, 1755
Mason, Sarah. Daughter of Daniel and Elizabeth,
born December 15, 1755
MacDaniel, Reuben. Son of James and Jean, born
November 22, 1755

Maccaboy, Elizabeth. Married James Givin,
                            October 5, 1755
MacCarty, Margaret. Married Stephen Hansford,
                            October 14, 1755
Mason, George. Married Elizabeth Durrest,
                            October 21, 1755
Maccullough, Sarah. Married John Ashby,
                            February 26, 1756
Murphy, Isaac. Married Catharine Ashby,
                            January 1, 1756
Million, Sarah Ann. Daughter of Robert and Keziah,
                            born February 13, 1756
Mays, Joseph. Son of Joseph and Sarah, born
                            April 18, 1756
Manuel, ———. Died at James Phillips,
                            September 10, 1753
Martyor, Margaret. Married John Lunsford,
                            June 6, 1756
More, Jane. Daughter of Nathaniel, born
                            June 17, 1756
Mananteer, Elijah. Son of Alexander, born
                            June 14, 1756
Montjoy, George. Son of William and Phillis, died
                            June 1, 1756
Mays, Robert. Married Elizabeth Bolling,
                            December 27, 1756

OVERWHARTON PARISH REGISTER. 129

Moore, Elizabeth. Daughter of William, born
December 23, 1756
Murphy, Lydia. Daughter of Isaac and Catharine,
born November 15, 1756
Monroe, John. Married Sarah Harrison,
September 23, 1756
Matheny, James. Son of James and Elizabeth, born
September 9, 1756
Maccullough, James. Son of Benjamin and Elizabeth,
born November 29, 1756
Mason, Lewis. Son of John, born February 5, 1757
Mason, Frances. Daughter of George, born
January 16, 1757
Mathews, Mary. Married James Turner,
March 3, 1757
Martin, Sarah. Married Moses Fletcher,
July 10, 1757
McCoy, Feanly. Married Jane Thomas, July 18, 1757
McCoy, Daniel. Son of Feanly, born
October 10, 1757
Mays, Benjamin. Son of William and Elizabeth,
born September 10, 1757
Mountjoy, George. Son of William and Phillis, born
September 1, 1757
Mays, George. Son of Joseph and Sarah, born
January 1, 1758

130 OVERWHARTON PARISH REGISTER.

Macinteer, Rodah. Was baptized April 9, 1758
Millian, Jeany. Daughter of Robert and Keziah, born
April 19, 1758
Moncure, Frances, Jr. Married Travers, Daniel, at "Claremont," October 7, 1762, by the Rev. Mr. James Scott
Moncure, William. Son of John and Ann, born
September 21, 1774
Matheny, William. Married Ann Sims,
September 10, 1747
Moses, Mary. Married Andrew Watson,
September 26, 1742
Monslow, John. Married Jean Waters,
October 26, 1748

N.

Norton, Elizabeth. Married Charles Colson,
February 1, 1739
Nelson, Margaret. Daughter of Alexander and
Margaret, born January 14, 1739
Nelson, Lettie. Daughter of Henry and Sarah, born
March 10, 1740
Nelson, Lettie. Daughter of Alexander, died
September 28, 1740
Nelson, Hannah. Daughter of John and Mary, born
October 19, 1740

Normand, James. Son of Thomas, born
September 13, 1740
Nelson, John. Married Mary Toby,
February 10, 1740
Normand, William. Son of Thomas and Martha,
born November 11, 1741
Nelson, Henry. Married Jean Goodwin,
October 18, 1742
Normand, George. Son of Thomas and Elizabeth,
born June 25, 1743
Nubal, Priscilla. Daughter of Samuel and Hannah,
born June 21, 1743
Nelson, William. Son of Henry and Jean, born
August 14, 1743
Nelson, Susannah. Daughter of Henry and Sarah,
born October 25, 1743
Nickolas, Elee. Married Nathaniel More,
December 31, 1743
Northcutt, Elizabeth. Married Anthony Philips,
December 26, 1743
Northcutt, Martha. Daughter of William and
Margery, born August 10, 1744
Nelson, Alexander. Married Margaret Butler,
February 21, 1745
Nelson, Henry. Son of Henry and Jean, born
August 2, 1745

132   OVERWHARTON PARISH REGISTER.

Nelson, John.   Married Sarah Whitson,
December 7, 1745
Newbold, William.   Son of Samuel and Joannah,
born December 12, 1745
Nelson, Alexander.   Departed this life,
October 19, 1745
Nelson, William.   Son of Alexander, born
February 2, 1746
Normand, Thomas.   Son of Thomas and Elizabeth,
born August 10, 1746
Nelson, Lydia.   Daughter of John and Sarah, born
September 24, 1746
Noble, Joshua.   Married Hannah Blackman,
September 7, 1746
Nelson, Frances.   Daughter of Henry and Sarah, born
January 15, 1747
Nelson, Jemima.   Daughter of Henry and Jane, born
January, 28, 1747
Nelson, John.   Was born July 10, 1747
Nelson, Mary.   Married John Mason,
November 27, 1747
Nowland, Richard.   Married Jane Wright,
December 20, 1747
Nelson, Elizabeth,   Was born October 9, 1747
Nelson, Margaret.   Married John Powwell,
September 4, 1748

OVERWHARTON PARISH REGISTER. 133

Nelson, John. Died at John Powwall's,
October 14, 1748
Nelson, Nanny. Daughter of John and Sarah, born
January 11, 1749
Nelson, Alexander. Son of Alexander and Mary,
born March 30, 1749
Nelson, Henry. Departed this life, February 29, 1749
Normand, Ann. Daughter of Thomas, born
February 14, 1750
Northcutt, Mary. Married Haswel Hardwick,
December 25, 1750
Nunn, Thomas. Son of John, born January 1, 1750–1
Nelson, Mary. Daughter of John and Sarah, born
March 2, 1751
Nelson, John. Son of Alexander, born March 5, 1751
Nelson, John. Son of Henry and Jane, born
May 21, 1751
Northcutt, Sarah. Married John Foxworthy,
December 25, 1751
Nubal, Sarah. Married Thomas Foxworthy,
September 29, 1751
Nicolas, John. Married Mary Hyden, April 23, 1752
Nickolas, John. Son of John, born
November 7, 1752
Nelson, Elizabeth. Married Daniel Mason,
January 30, 1753

Nelson, Margaret. Daughter of Alexander and
                            Margaret, born January 10, 1753
Nickson, Patty. Daughter of John and Rachel, born
                            October 2, 1754
Nowland, Jean. Married John Brown,
                            August 24, 1755
Nelson, George. Son of Alexander and Margaret,
                            born December 4, 1755
Nelson, Jesse. Son of John and Sarah, born
                            January 22, 1756
Noble, Joshua. Son of Joshua and Hannah, born
                            August 17, 1756
Noble, Jean. Married Derby Driscal,
                            October 4, 1756
Noxal, Saxfield. Married Ann Boning,
                            August 1, 1757
Nelson, Jean. Daughter of John, born
                            January 24, 1758
Nelson, Alexander. Departed this life,
                            June 20, 1758

O.

Onsby, Elizabeth. Married Carty Wells,
                            September 10, 1738
O'Cane, John. The son of Derby and Susanna, born
                            March 20, 1739

O'Neal, Timothy. Married Elizabeth Mathews,
April 22, 1739
O'Cane, Derby. Married Susannah Smith,
December 16, 1739
O'Cane, Thomas. Son of Derby, born May 4, 1740
O'Daneal, Priscilla. Daughter of Timothy and
Elizabeth, born April 1, 1743
O'Cane, Mary. Daughter of Susannah and Derby,
born May 9, 1745
Oram, Rachel. Married John Hart, March 23, 1746
O'Daneal, Elizabeth. Married William Thornberry,
July 10, 1746
O'Cain, James. Son of Derby and Susannah, born
October 4, 1747
Ogiloy, John. Married Margaret Murray,
October 7, 1750
Ogiloy, Ann. Daughter of John, born April 27, 1750
O'Cain, Daniel. Son of Derby and Susannah, born
April 1, 1750
Osbon, Judith. Daughter of William, born
February 2, 1751
O'Cain, Derby. Son of Derby, born March 4, 1753
Ogiloy, Winifred. Daughter of John, born
July 18, 1751
Ogiloy, Margaret. Daughter of Margaret and John,
born April 3, 1754

O'Banion, Ann.   Married Alexander Farrow,
                                        October 5, 1753
Owendowney, John.   Died at Priscilla Hays',
                                        January 22, 1754
Oliver, Keziah.   Daughter of John and Mary, born
                                        April 5, 1754
O'Cain, Henry.   Son of Derby and Susannah, born
                                        August 4, 1755
O'Daneal, James.   Married Theodsian Congers,
                                        October 19, 1755
O'Daneal, William Scott.   Son of James and
                            Theodsian, born August 10, 1756

P.

Powel, John.   Son of Charles and Elizabeth, born
                                        September 20, 1731
Powel, Peter.   Son of Charles and Elizabeth, born
                                        February 17, 1733
Powell, Elizabeth.   Daughter of Charles and
                            Elizabeth, born April 26, 1735
Powel, Martha.   Daughter of Charles and Elizabeth
                            born September 26, 1736
Pettigrew, James.   Son of John and Mary, born
                                        April 2, 1737
Pepper, Mary.   Married James Suddeth,
                                        May 13, 1738

OVERWHARTON PARISH REGISTER. 137

Parker, Martha. Married Peter Bailen,
August 6, 1738
Pritchet, Philip's wife, Elizabeth, died
January 29, 1739
Peddicoat, Jannet. Married Moses Rowley,
May 16, 1739
Prim, John. Married Margaret Welch,
September 9, 1739
Peddicoat, John. Son of John and Mary, born
December 28, 1739
Powton, Edward. Married Mary Matheney,
November 20, 1739
Pattin, William. Married Joyie Mcinteer,
January 27, 1740
Porter, Thomas. Departed this life,
February 26, 1740
Payton, Catharine. Married William Scrogging,
February 18, 1740
Powel, Charles. Son of Charles and Elizabeth, born
May 26, 1740
Prim, William. Son of John and Margaret, born
July 28, 1740
Payton, Alexander. Married Jane Heffermon,
May 20, 1740
Phips, Stephen. Married Rosamond Mayow,
June 1, 1740

Paddeth, Thomas.   Son of James and Elizabeth, died
                                            February 8, 1741
Patten, Margaret.   Daughter of William and Joyie,
                                        born March 10, 1741
Peyton, Elizabeth.   Daughter of John and Eleanor,
                                          born July 1, 1741
Perry, Mary.   Daughter of Prudence, born
                                            July 21, 1741
Philips, James.   Married Elizabeth Griffin,
                                        September 27, 1741
Philips, Lettie.   Daughter of James and Elizabeth,
                                     born November 22, 1741
Punton, Edward.   Departed this life, January 22, 1741
Payton, William.   Son of John, born July 25, 1742
Pritchet, William.   Married Jane Cook,
                                          January 26, 1742
Pritchet, Philip.   Married Catharine Cole,
                                          January 24, 1742
Pritchet, Anne.   Daughter of Philip and Catharine,
                                     born September 4, 1742
Pattin, Jean.   Daughter of William and Jean, born
                                         December 23, 1742
Peyton, Henry.   Son of John and Eleanor, born
                                            March 9, 1743
Pike, Margary.   Died at Michael Pike's,
                                         February 27, 1744

Payton, Rachel   Daughter of John and Worth, born
August 22, 1743
Philips, Anthony.   Married Elizabeth Northcutt,
December 26, 1743
Pritchet, Catharine.   Daughter of Philip, born
December 28, 1743
Powel, Peggy.   Daughter of Charles and Betty, born
April 8, 1744
Powel, Charles,   Departed this life, April 30, 1744
Pritchet, Lewis.   Married Mary Littimore,
March 31, 1744
Poole, Sarah.   Married John Foley, December 11, 1744
Philips, William.   Son of James and Elizabeth, born
November 1, 1744
Pritchet, Philip, Sr.   Departed this life,
November 14, 1744
Pownall, Elizabeth.   Married John Cooper,
March 30, 1745
Powtone, Isabel.   Daughter of Mary, born
February 9, 1745
Philips, Dorcas.   Daughter of Anthony and Elizabeth,
born March 10, 1745
Philips, William.   Son of John and Mary, born
February 2, 1745
Perender, Eleanor.   Married Thomas Massey,
June 26, 1745

Parson, Sarah. Daughter of Anne and William, born
May 26, 1745
Powell, Elizabeth. Married Duke Whalbone,
December 3, 1745
Plummer, Mary. Married Richard Matthis,
October 5, 1745
Philips, Mary. Daughter of Robert and Elizabeth,
died October 16, 1745
Page, Sarah. Married Nathaniel More,
September 11, 1745
Porter, Howsen. Married John Stark,
January 1, 1746
Powel, Richard. Son of Mary, born
February 14, 1746
Prim, Anne. Daughter of John and Margaret, born
September 15, 1746
Payton, Charles. Son of John and Werth, born
November 1, 1746
Proctor, Edward. Married Anny Weeks,
February 15, 1747
Porch, Robert. Departed this life April 5, 1747
Peyton, Anne. Married Thomas Harrison,
July 2, 1747
Peyton, Eleanor. Wife of John, died October 5, 1747
Pumphrey, Elizabeth. Married Morthough McCaboy,
December 27, 1747

OVERWHARTON PARISH REGISTER. 141

Patten, Ann. Daughter of William, born
                                December 23, 1747
Phillips, Mary. Daughter of James Philips, born
                                January 15, 1748
Patten, Ann. Daughter of William, died
                                January 11, 1748
Pritchett, Lewis. Son of Lewis and Mary, born
                                February 17, 1748
Powell, Renn. Son of Mary, born February 2, 1748
Pane, Francis. Son of Francis, born March 18, 1748
Pane, Francis. Son of Francis, died April 15, 1748
Patterson, John. Was born May 8, 1748
Peyton, Elizabeth. Daughter of John, died
                                May 11, 1748
Pully, Robert. Married Mary Thomson,
                                August 28, 1748
Price, William. Married Sarah Allenthrop,
                                August 8, 1748
Petter, John. Married Judith Lunsford,
                                February 27, 1748
Pearson, Hannah. Departed this life,
                                November 12, 1748
Porch, Thomas. Married Rachel Limbrick,
                                July 22, 1748
Punell, Emmeal. Son of Richard and Mary,
                                July 20, 1748

Peyton, Philip.   Married Winifred Bussel,
September 15, 1748
Pownall, John.   Married Margaret Nelson,
September 4, 1748
Pilcher, Stephen.   Married Lucy Clarke,
November 7, 1748
Parsons, Ann.   Departed this life,
November 26, 1748
Pownall, Margaret.   Daughter of John, born
November 10, 1748
Peyton, Valentine.   Son of Philip and Winifred, born
March 19, 1749
Pattison, Sarah, alias Congers.   Married Thomas
Hampton, January 1, 1749
Pannel, Mary.   Died at William Patton's,
October 25, 1749
Porter, Calvert.   Married Elizabeth Cash,
Sepember 21, 1749
Porter, Joseph.   Son of Calvert and Elizabeth, born
October 21, 1749
Patton, Sarah.   Daughter of William, born
November 24, 1749
Pilcher, Samuel.   Son of Stephen and Elizabeth, born
January 5, 1750
Pilcher, Elizabeth.   Departed this life,
January 23, 1750

Pilcher, James. Son of Stephen, born
February 17, 1750
Payne, Edward. Married Ann Holland Congers,
February 27, 1750
Paterson, Behethelan. Daughter of Mary, born
April 17, 1750
Pyke, Ann. Married Henry Hurst,
March 20, 1750
Peyton, Jeremiah. Son of John and Werth, born
January 29, 1750
Prim, John. Son of John and Margaret, born
May 17, 1750
Pilcher, Stephen. Married Bridget MacConchie,
December 1, 1750
Powell, Mary. Died at William Hendale's,
November 21, 1750
Pattison, Susannah. Married James Mings,
September 7, 1750
Phillips, Dianah. Daughter of Anthony and
Elizabeth, born February 22, 1751
Pattison, Lydia Alvin. Daughter of Elizabeth, born
May 4, 1751
Payton, Nancy. Daughter of John and Werth, born
November 13, 1751
Peyton, John. Married Elizabeth Waller,
November 17, 1751

Prim, Thomas. Son of John and Margaret, born
December 13, 1751
Porter, Calvert. Son of Calvert and Elizabeth, born
March 1, 1752
Powel, John. Married Margaret MacDaniel,
February 10, 1752
Phillips, Dianah. Departed this life,
February 20, 1752
Porch, Rachel. Married William Burton,
October 7, 1753
Powel, Jemima. Daughter of John and Margaret,
born November 9, 1753
Petter, Jane. Daughter of John and Judith, born
December 11, 1753
Porch, Ann. Married William Berry, February 26, 1754
Porter, Thomas. Son of Calvert and Elizabeth, born
January 11, 1754
Peirson, Nanny. Daughter of William and Sarah,
born January 18, 1754
Pilcher, Mary. Died at Alexander Macanteer's,
January 25, 1754
Porter, John. Departed this life, July 14, 1754
Parinder, Elizabeth. Married William Adie,
July 25, 1754
Peyton, John Rousey. Son of John, baptized
November 17, 1754

OVERWHARTON PARISH REGISTER. 145

Peyton, Dr. Valentine. Departed this life,
November 28, 1754
Patten, John and William. Sons of William and
Joyie, born December 28, 1754
Powell, Patty. Daughter of John and Margaret, born
November 17, 1755
Patterson, Ruth. Daughter of Mary, born
September 19, 1755
Porter, Frances. Daughter of Calvert and Elizabeth,
born January 12, 1756
Porter, Thomas. Was baptized February 23, 1756
Powell, Martha. Married John Goldsmith,
January 19, 1756
Porter, Joseph. Married Jemima Smith,
February 24, 1756
Patten, William. Married Isabella Kennedy,
December 19, 1756
Philips, Lettie. Married John Cummings,
February 21, 1757
Porter Charity. Daughter of Calvert and Elizabeth,
born Septenber 9, 1757
Pilford, Elizabeth. Married William Cooper,
January 5, 1758
Peyton, John. Married Susannnah Lunsford,
March 28, 1758

Q.

Quidley, Stephen.   Son of William, died
                                    February 8, 1745

R.

Robison, Philip.   Married Margaret Spoldin,
                                    November 26, 1738
Ross, Rebecca.   Daughter of William and Margaret,
                                    born February 28, 1739
Rowley, Moses.   Married Jannet Peddicoat,
                                    May 16, 1739
Rout, Hannah.   Daughter of Peter and Martha, born
                                    January 31, 1740
Renny, John.   Married Mary Linton, April 6, 1740
Richards, John.   Married Mary Latham,
                                    January 24, 1740
Renny, Jeremiah.   Son of John and Mary, born
                                    November 18, 1740
Robinson, John.   Son of Benjamin and Catharine,
                                    born December 22, 1740
Reddish, Jean.   Daughter of Robert, born
                                    January 8, 1741
Robinson, Mary.   Daughter of Christopher and
                                    Eleanor, born January 1, 1741
Robinson, Sarah.   Married John Kirke,
                                    June 23, 1741

Richards, Francis. Son of John and Mary, born
May 25, 1741
Renny, Jacob. Son of William and Barbara, born
August 27, 1741
Raper, Susanna. Daughter of Thomas and Elizabeth,
born September 30, 1741
Rogers, William. Son of Rachel, born
June 1, 1742
Rogers, William. Son of Richard and Mary, born
October 13, 1741
Ross, John. Son of William and Margaret, born
June 4, 1742
Routt, John. Son of Peter and Martha, born
December 13, 1742
Renny, Prisly. Son of John and Mary, born
December 28, 1742
Rassan, William. Married Priscilla Manzey,
October 27, 1743
Robinson, Nanny. Daughter of Benjamin and
Catharine, born April 23, 1743
Reaves, George. Married Anne Webster,
April 3, 1743
Robinson, Ann. Married William Green,
December 18, 1743
Robinson, Christopher. Son of Christopher and
Eleanor, born February 25, 1744

Rush, Benjamin. Married Alice Grigsby,
April 1, 1744
Ross, John. Son of William and Margaret, died
September 4, 1744
Rice, Lydia. Daughter of John and Ann, born
November 9, 1744
Raper, Elizabeth. Daughter of Frances, died
October 12, 1744
Richards, Francis. Son of John, died
November 8, 1744
Renny, Tabitha. Daughter of John and Mary, born
March 8, 1745
Routt, James. Son of Peter and Martha, born
July 29, 1745
Ryley, Thomas. Son of John and Elizabeth, born
July 12, 1745
Reynolds, Peter. Married Easter Carr, June 2, 1745
Rhodes, Mary. Married Isaac Basriet,
May 18, 1745
Ryan, William. Son of Michael and Winefred, died
December 4, 1745
Robinson, Christopher, Jr. Died December 8, 1745
Ransdell, Elizabeth. Daughter of Wharton and
Margaret, born April 6, 1746
Regnold, James. Married Margaret Deckon,
August 19, 1746

Rhodes, Sanford.   Son of John and Martha, born
December 13, 1746
Robinson, William.   Son of Christopher and Eleanor,
born November 3, 1746
Rosser, Sarah.   Married Hayward Todd,
September 7, 1746
Robinson, Rebecca.   Married William Godfrey,
October 26, 1746
Radcliffe, Eleanor.   Married Thomas Turner,
September 13, 1746
Rayle, Hugh.   Son of John, born February 24, 1747
Richetts, Sarah Ann.   Daughter of Thomas, born
September 21, 1747
Raper, John.   Son of Elizabeth, born June 26, 1747
Renny, Calab.   Son of John and Mary, born
May 20, 1747
Ryan, Daniel.   Son of Michael and Winifred, born
September 2, 1747
Robertson, John.   Married Rose Jones,
October 15, 1747
Robe, Isabel.   Married Thomas Weddell,
January 3, 1748
Read, Mary.   Daughter of Robert and Dorothy, born
January 5, 1748
Rhodes, Martha.   The wife of John, died
April 7, 1748

Ryan, Daniel. Son of Michael and Winifred, died
March 7, 1748
Read, Mary. Was baptized March 13, 1748
Robinson, Mary. The wife of Henry, died
March 26, 1748
Ramsdell, Edward. Son of Wharton, born
June 19, 1748
Read, John. Married Ann Sebastian, July 21, 1748
Rhodes, John. Departed this life, November 12, 1748
Robinson, Elizabeth. Married John Rabbing,
December 29, 1748
Rabbing, John. Married Elizabeth Robinson,
December 29, 1748
Robinson, Sarah. Married James Fernsley,
November 3, 1748
Robinson, Josham. Married John Sprayburry,
November 9, 1748
Robinson, James. Son of Christopher and Eleanor,
born April 16, 1749
Ryley, John. Son of John and Elizabeth, born
March 4, 1749
Rabbing, John. Died at William Kinz's,
February 4, 1749
Routt, Betty. Daughter of Peter, died June 27, 1749
Renny, Lydia. Daughter of John and Mary, born
July 30, 1749

Rice, John. Departed this life, September 2, 1749
Reiliegh, Ann. Departed this life,
  September 24, 1749
Robinson, Benjamin. Married Sarah Stacy,
  January 2, 1750
Redman, Ann. Daughter of Patrick, born
  December 7, 1749
Robinson, Nathaniel. Son of Benjamin and Sarah,
  born April 22, 1750
Ransdell, Wharton. Son of Wharton and Margaret,
  born January 12, 1750
Robinson, Henry. Married Winifred Bailis,
  August 1, 1750
Ross, William. Son of William and Margaret, born
  September 11, 1750
Risen, John. Married Hannah Chinn,
  October 20, 1750
Ryley, Charles. Son of John and Elizabeth, born
  October 11, 1750
Reeds, Elizabeth. Married William Spilman,
  February, 25, 1751
Runnils, Frank. Died March 1C, 1751
Renny, Butler. Son of John and Mary, born
  April 18, 1751
Redman, Sarah. Daughter of Patrick, born
  April 16, 1752

Riley, Nanny.   Daughter of Nickolas, born
April 17, 1752
Rhodes, Ann.   Married Robert Fristoe,
February 23, 1752
Robinson, Carty.   Daughter of Benjamin and Sarah,
born January 8, 1752
Rankins, Ann.   Daughter of George and Sarah, born
January 14, 1752
Rounde, David.   Married Mary Turner,
January 28, 1753
Ryley, George.   Son of John and Elizabeth, born
February 28, 1753
Rose, William.   Married Sarah Grigsby,
June 5, 1753
Renny, John.   Son of John and Mary, born
November 8, 1753
Raleigh, Henry.   Son of Nickolas and Winifred, born
November 21, 1753
Ryley, George.   Son of John and Elizabeth, died
October 5, 1753
Routt, William.   Married Winifred Byram,
November 27, 1753
Riding, Thomas.   Son of James and Mary, born
April 27, 1753
Read, John.   Married Margaret Allenthrop,
March 5, 1754

OVERWHARTON PARISH REGISTER.   153

Randal, Catharine. Married George Bussel,
January 8, 1754
Robinson, George. Son of Sarah and Benjamin, born
February 7, 1754
Redman, John. Son of Patrick and Elizabeth, born
July 18, 1754
Routt, Peter. Son of William and Winifred, born
October 22, 1754
Richards, John. Married Susannah Thomas Heath,
March 6, 1754
Richetts, Sarah Ann. Daughter of Thomas and
Sarah, baptized January 26, 1755
Riggins, Bridget. Married John Flitter,
March 16, 1755
Robinson, Simon. Married Mary Jack,
August 3, 1755
Robinson, Benjamin. Married Elizabeth Stacey,
May 25, 1755
Roach, Thomas. Married Ann Cooke,
December 28, 1755
Richards, Elizabeth. Was baptized
January 26, 1756
Ryley, James. Son of Nickolas and Winifred, born
January 21, 1756
Robinson, Lishea. Daughter of Benjamin and Sarah,
born February 25, 1756

Routt, William. Son of William and Winifred, born
May 29, 1756
Rigg, Lewis. Son of John and Betty, born
March 17, 1757
Rowels, Jesse. Son of Henry and Isabell, born
January 28, 1757
Renny, Sennot. Son of John and Mary, born
February 25, 1757
Ryley, Betty. Daughter of Nickolas and Winifred,
born March 20, 1757
Reiley, Mary. Daughter of John and Elizabeth, born
March 20, 1757
Raper, Elizabeth. Married Alexander Sutor,
May 8, 1757
Ryan, Michael. Departed this life,
October 10, 1757
Ross, William. Departed this life, December 26, 1757
Rose, William. Married Jane Grigsby,
March 14, 1758
Robinson, Benjamin. Son of Benjamin and Sarah,
born June 21, 1758
Riddle, Thomas. Married Bridget Amely,
February 5, 1758
Roath, Patrick. Married Elizabeth Wise,
October 9, 1742

OVERWHARTON PARISH REGISTER. 155

S.

Stark, Sarah. Daughter of James and Elizabeth, born
August 23, 1731
Stark, Jean. Daughter of James and Elizabeth, born
February 1, 1733
Stark, Anne. Daughter of James and Elizabeth, born
February 9, 1736
Stark, Benjamin. Son of James and Elizabeth, born
September 27, 1738
Suddeth, James. Married Mary Pepper, May 13, 1738
Strother, Elizabeth. Married John Frogg,
November 9, 1738
Spoldin, Margaret. Married Philip Robinson,
November 26, 1738
Smith, Elizabeth. Married Charles Cornish,
December 17, 1738
Simpson, Mary. Departed this life,
January 15, 1739
Scott, Helen. Daughter of James and Sarah, born
June 7, 1739
Smith, Susannah. Married Derby O'Cain,
December 16, 1739
Stuart, William. Son of James and Mary, born
January 1, 1740
Scogging, William. Married Catharine Payton,
February 18, 1740

Stuart, James. Married Mary Dunaway,
February 12, 1740
Simpson, Million. Daughter of William and Diana,
born May 5, 1740
Strong, John. Son of Nathaniel and Mary, born
June 22, 1740
Smith, Withers and George. Sons of Nathaniel and
Elizabeth, born June 13, 1740
Sinclair, George. Son of George and Winifred, born
November 7, 1740
Scott, Alexander. Son of James and Sarah, born
July 10, 1740
Simpson, John. Married Silent Johnston,
August 17, 1740
Smith, William. Son of Henry and Sarah, died
September 17, 1740
Sinclair, George. Departed this life,
January 12, 1741
Sinclair, Margaret. Married Francis Tennel,
November 9, 1740
Scott, Sarah. Daughter of Rev. James Scott, born
January 22, 1741
Smith, Henry. Son of Henry and Sarah, born
February 3, 1741
Stacey, Simon. Married Judith Tolson,
August 22, 1741

Stanly, Marjory. Married Edmond Webster,
            November 20, 1741
Short, Jean. The wife of John, died
            December 9, 1741
Sturdy, Margaret. Married Parish Garner,
            January 21, 1741
Scott, James. Son of Rev. James and Sarah, born
            January 8, 1742
Smith, Mary. Married William Cammel,
            July 25, 1742
Stacey, Sarah. Daughter of Judith and Simon, born
            August 20, 1742
Stuart, James. Son of Mary and James, born
            October 26, 1742
Sinclair, Winifred. Daughter of George and
            Winifred, born October 3, 1742
Stuart, William. Died at Mr. Scott's,
            October 22, 1742
Sinclair, Winifred. Wife of George, died
            October 22, 1742
Spinks, Enoch. Son of John and Rosamond, born
            November 10, 1742
Smith, William. Son of Henry and Sarah, born
            October 28, 1742
Sturdy, Elizabeth. Daughter of Robert and
            Elizabeth died November 20, 1742

Smith, Temple. Son of Nathaniel, died
January 24, 1743
Smith, Susannah. Married John Cotton,
February 17, 1743
Simmonds, Jemima. Daughter of George and
Elizabeth, born March 17, 1743
Stacey, Katharine. Daughter of Elizabeth, born
March 17, 1743
Smith, Anne. Daughter of Robert and Phillis, born
May 21, 1743
Simpson, Alexander. Married Catharine Fant,
July 17, 1743
Sinclair, Clementina. Daughter of George, died
July 21, 1743
Stungfellow, Benjamin. Married Mary Foley,
June 15, 1743
Shaw, John. Married Mary Waters,
June 12, 1743
Simpson, Elizabeth. Married John Whitcomb,
November 24, 1743
Spoldin, Francis. Son of Thomas and Elizabeth,
born January 7, 1743
Smith, Mary. Married John Montgomery,
January 16, 1744
Strother, Margaret. Married George Molton,
April 6, 1744

Stacey, Benjamin. Son of Simon and Judith, born
April 7, 1744
Suthard, Rose. Married Silent Jeffreys,
January 19, 1744
Suddeth, Mary. Married Edward Boling, May 4, 1744
Shorter, Anne. Married Francis Tyler, May 17, 1744
Sinclair, Patience. Married William Young,
July 23, 1744
Stark, Daniel. Son of James and Elizabeth, born
May 30, 1744
Simpson, Priscilla. Daughter of George and
Margaret, born September 26, 1744
Savage, Eleanor. Married John Hogg,
December 19, 1744
Smith, Temple. Son of Nathaniel, born
April 26, 1745
Suddeth, Lawrence. Married Dorothy West,
April 18, 1745
Scott, Christian. Daughter of James and Sarah, born
March 4, 1745
Smith, Susannah. Daughter of Robert and Phillis,
born April 16, 1745
Suddeth, Henry. Married Mary Latham,
June 25, 1745
Suddeth, Sarah. Married Thomas Griffin,
July 18, 1745

OVERWHARTON PARISH REGISTER.

Suddeth, Ann. Daughter of Benjamin and Silent,
born July 17, 1745
Suitor, Alexander. Married Margaret Issac,
July 21, 1745
Sullivant, Mary. Married Peter Gowing, May 28, 1745
Stacey, Catharine. Married William Hill,
September 17, 1745
Smith, George. Son of Henry and Sarah, born
October 19, 1745
Suddeth, Elizabeth. Daughter of Lawrence and
Dorothy, born November 3, 1745
Simson, Elizabeth. Daughter of Alexander and
Catharine, born January 4, 1746
Spoore, Ann. Departed this life, January 29, 1746
Stark, John. Married Howson Porter,
February 1, 1746
Stark, Jeremiah. Married Tabitha Lowry,
January 29, 1747
Sayas, William. Son of Richard and Ann, born
March 10, 1747
Stone, Josias. Son of Josias and Mary, born
June 17, 1747
Sanderson, William. Son of John and Jean, born
June 7, 1747
Sims, Ann. Married William Matheny,
September 10, 1747

Smith, Martha. Daughter of Robert, born
  November 3, 1747
Smith, Christian. Daughter of John and Catharine,
  born December 2, 1747
Stark, James. Son of James and Catharine, born
  December 21, 1747
Simpson, Mary. Daughter of Alexander, born
  December 10, 1747
Smith, John. Married Elizabeth Hornbuckle,
  December 3, 1747
Simson, Susannah. Daughter of George and
  Margaret, born January 18, 1748
Suddeth, Margaret. Daughter of Benjamin and
  Silent, born January 12, 1748
Stark, Lydia. Daughter of James, born June 31, 1748
Sebastian, Ann. Married John Read, July 21, 1748
Smith, Daniel and Sarah. Children of Henry,
  baptized October 24, 1748
Smith, Sarah. Daughter of Henry, died
  October 29, 1748
Sprayburry, John. Married Joshan Robinson,
  November 9, 1748
Stark, John. Son of Jeremima and Tabitha, born
  November 6, 1748
Stacey, Silvia. Daughter of John, Jr., born
  December 6, 1748

Smith, Catharine. Married Joshua Kendal,
April 4, 1749
Stone, Betty. Daughter of Josias and Mary, born
April 14, 1749
Stacey, Mary. Daughter of Judy and Simon, born
February 15, 1749
Sprayburry, James. Son of John and Joshan, born
June 14, 1749
Sanderson, John. Son of John and Jean, born
August 2, 1749
Somacks, Richard. Died at John Peyton's, Aquia,
August 28, 1749
Stark, Elizabeth. Daughter of John and Howson,
born August 16, 1749
Suddeth, Grace. Daughter of Lawrence and Dorothy,
born September 23, 1749
Sturdy, Robert. Departed this life,
November 3, 1749
Stark, Sarah Ann. Daughter of James and Catharine,
born November 25, 1749
Stephens, Mary. Died at Edward Balls,
January 18, 1750
Stacey, Sarah. Married Benjamin Robinson,
January 2, 1750
Smith, Sith. Daughter of Robert and Phillis, born
January 10, 1750

OVERWHARTON PARISH REGISTER. 163

Suddeth, Catharine. Daughter of Benjamin, born
                                March 27, 1750
Suddeth, Catharine. Departed this life,
                                  April 11, 1750
Spolding, Sarah. Daughter of Thomas and Sarah,
                                born March 4, 1750
Simpson, Jane. Daughter of John and Elizabeth,
                              born January 27, 1750
Smith, William. Married Betty Barbee,
                                January 1, 1750
Sylva, John. Married Bridget Cooper,
                                    July 1, 1750
Smith, Enoch. Son of Henry and Sarah, born
                                 June 21, 1750
Simms, Richard. Married Betty Bridwell,
                                October 15, 1750
Strother, Margaret. Married John Murdock,
                                October 26, 1750
Sylvy, Nancy   Daughter of John, born
                                October 22, 1750
Stacey, Peggy. Daughter of John and Elizabeth,
                            born September 14, 1750
Simpson, Sarah. Daughter of Alexander, born
                              December 13, 1750
Slaughter, Robert. Married Susanna Harrison,
                              December 11, 175C

164 OVERWHARTON PARISH REGISTER.

Sinclair, George. Died at Hannah Bailis',
January 12, 1751
Spilman, William. Married Elizabeth Reeds,
February 25, 1751
Selden, Samuel. Married Mary Thompson Mason,
April 11, 1751
Sinclair, Elizabeth. Married Charles Jones,
April 21, 1751
Suddeth, William. Son of Benjamin and Silent, born
March 7, 1751
Stone, Valentine. Son of Josiah, baptized
April 30, 1751
Stacey, Dorothy. Wife of John, Sr., died
February 5, 1751
Sebastian, William. Married Sarah Kelly,
June 11, 1751
Stanard, Elizabeth. Married William Howard,
May 29, 1751
Sanderson, Thomas. Son of John, born
May 2, 1751
Stringfellow, Mary. Married William Bouchard,
May 12, 1751
Spilman, Thomas. Son of William and Elizabeth,
born November 29, 1751
Selden, Miles Carey. Son of Samuel and Mary, born
November 28, 1751

OVERWHARTON PARISH REGISTER. 165

Stark, Sarah. Daughter of Howson and John, born
January 29, 1752
Smith, Sarah. Daughter of Henry and Sarah, born
January 20, 1752
Suddeth, Lawence. Son of James and Hannah, born
February 21, 1752
Smith, Nathaniel. Son of Robert and Phillis, born
March 19, 1752
Shadborn, Frances Ann. Daughter of Jane, born
April 23, 1752
Stark, Jeremiah. Son of James, born
June 11, 1752
Smith, Elizabeth. Wife of Nathaniel, died
April 25, 1752
Smith, Lydia. Married Peter Hansbrough,
May 27, 1752
Spoldin, Elizabeth. Daughter of Thomas, born
May 22, 1752
Smith, Richard. Married Susanna Davis,
November 17, 1752
Smith, Mary. Married Michael Dial,
November 19, 1752
Sturdy, William, Married Phillis Jones,
December 17, 1752
Simmons, Keziah. Married William Boning,
February 4, 1753

Sullivan, Sarah. Married George Hinson,
February 4, 1753
Sanderson, Sarah. Daughter of John, born
February 21, 1753
Stone, Mary. Daughter of Josias and Mary, born
April 28, 1753
Sims, James. Son of Richard, born April 16, 1753
Selden, Samuel. Son of Samuel and Mary, born
March 20, 1753
Selden, Samuel. Departed this life, April 19, 1753
Suddeth, Susannah. Daughter of Benjamin and
Mary, born, April 25, 1753
Suddeth, Moses. The son of Joseph and Jemima,
born July 28, 1753
Smith, Ann. Wife of Thomas, died July 20, 1753,
aged 108 years
Stark, Mary. Daughter of Tabitha and Jeremiah,
born May 19, 1753
Shamlin, Martha. Married John Gunn,
September 30, 1758
Scoulcraft, James. Married Margaret Mills,
October 14, 1753
Smith, John. Departed this life,
September 23, 1753
Selman, William. Son of Benjamin and Ann, born
November 19, 1753

Shoemake, Spencer. Son of William and Ann, born
November 26, 1753
Syloy, Sulky. Daughter of John and Bridget, born
February 20, 1754
Scoulcraft, Mary. Daughter of James and Margaret,
born March 11, 1754
Smith, Sarah. Daughter of Parker and Catharine,
born February 28, 1754
Stark, James. Departed this life, April 12, 1754
Sturdy, Joanna. Married Rowley Lunsford,
June 16, 1754
Stacey, Suky. Daughter of John and Elizabeth, born
July 10, 1754
Smith, Thomas. Son of Henry and Sarah, born
October 4, 1754
Smith, Margaret. Married Joseph Jeffries,
October 24, 1754
Sanderson, Jenny. Daughter of John and Jean, born
December 10, 1754
Selden, Mary Mason. Daughter of Samuel and Mary,
born October 1, 1754
Stark, William. Son of John and Howson, born
December 14, 1754
Simson, Elizabeth. Married David Bradly, Apr. 17, 1755
Spilman, Jeremiah. Married Bridget Edwards,
January 16, 1755

168   *OVERWHARTON PARISH REGISTER.*

Smith, Susanna.   Daughter of Richard and Elizabeth,
born January 20, 1755
Stark, Howson.   Wife of John, died April 11, 1755
Sprayburry, John.   Son of John and Joshan, baptized
April 20, 1755
Smith, Rosamond.   Married William Hammet,
May 6, 1755
Skaines, Mary.   Married David Macquatty,
May 6, 1755
Stacey, Elizabeth.   Married Benjamin Robinson, Jr.,
May 25, 1755
Stacey, Peter.   Married Ruth Croscuel, May 25, 1755
Smith, Banister and Susannah Banister Smith.   Were
baptized July 6, 1755
Summers, Elizabeth.   Married John Taylor,
November 8, 1755
Simpson, Franky.   Daughter of Alexander and
Catharine, born November 13, 1755
Stone, Philadelphia.   Daughter of Mary and Josias,
born September 22, 1755
Smith, Thomas.   Married Mary Ann Williams,
February 21, 1756
Smith, Jemima.   Married Joseph Porter,
February 26, 1756
Selden, Samuel.   Son of Samuel and Mary, born
April 30, 1756

Simpson, William. Married Lettie Lunsford,
January 18, 1756
Silvy, Phobe. Daughter of John and Bridget, born
March 21, 1756
Sodarth, Sarah. Daughter of Joseph, baptized
April 13, 1756
Stacey, Shadrick. Son of John and Elizabeth, born
August 20, 1756
Shumate, William. Son of Ann and William, born
August 11, 1756
Stark, John. Married Hannah Eaves, May 29, 1756
Suddeth, Jane. Daughter of James and Hannah, born
May 18, 1756
Smith, Joseph. Son of Henry and Sarah, born
June 6, 1756
Sutherland, Dr. John. Married Susannah Brent,
September 15, 1756
Strother, Alice. Married Robert Washington,
December 16, 1756
Smith, Phillis. Married John Green,
December 19, 1756
Stark, James. Son of John and Hannah, born
February 7, 1757
Stacey, Sarah. Married Isaker Edwards, May 16, 1757
Sutor, Alexander. Married Elizabeth Raper,
May 8, 1757

Smith, John. Married Elizabeth Welit,
December 7, 1757
Sumate, Lettie. Daughter of William and Ann, born
February 5, 1757
Suddeth, Priscilla. Was baptized October 23, 1757
Smith, Sarah. Daughter of John, born
January 24, 1758
Smith, Mary. Married James Hardage Lane,
January 12, 1758
Selden, Mary. Wife of Samuel, Departed this life,
January 5, 1758
Smith, William. Son of Thomas and Mary Ann,
born January 24, 1758
Simpson, Sarah. Daughter of William and Lettie,
born June 25, 1758

T.

Turner, Margaret. Daughter of Henry and Mary,
born June 1, 1733
Turner, Betty. Daughter of Henry and Mary, born
May 28, 1736
Traverse, Peter Daniel. Married ———
Traverse, Sarah. Married Peter Daniel, July 15, 1736
Tyler, Margaret. Married William Waugh,
September 10, 1738
Taylor, Catharine. Married William Chimp,
January 31, 1739

OVERWHARTON PARISH REGISTER. 171

Taylor, Elizabeth. Daughter of Henry, born
July 25, 1740
Trewick, Eleanor. Daughter of Robert, died
May 19, 1740, aged 8 years
Tunnel, Francis. Married Margaret Sinclair,
November 9, 1740
Trewick, Elizabeth. Daughter of Robert and
Marjory, born December 24, 1740
Toby, Mary. Married John Nelson,
February 10, 1740
Tolson, Judith. Married Simon Stacey,
August 22, 1741
Turner, Alexander. Son of Edward and Jean, born
July 25, 1741
Tunnel, Joseph. Son of Francis and Margaret, born
February 18, 1742
Thompson, Robert. Married Catharine Tomlinson,
September 1, 1742
Tomlinson, Catharine. Married Robert Thompson,
September 1, 1742
Turner, Hannah. Daughter of Henry and Mary,
born October 30, 1742
Trewick, Eleanor. Daughter of Robert and Marjory,
born January 24, 1743
Tyler, John. Son of Henry and Else, born
April 17, 1743

Tomison, Richard and William. Sons of Simon
    and Barbara, born August 21, 1743
Tyler Frances. Married Anne Strother, May 17, 1744
Taylor, John. Son of John and Eleanor, born
    December 1, 1745
Turner, Sarah. Departed this life, December 25, 1744
Tomison, Jane. Daughter of Simon and Barbara,
    born November 17, 1745
Thornberry, William. Married Elizabeth O'Daneal,
    July 10, 1746
Todd, Hayward. Married Sarah Rosser,
    September 7, 1746
Turner, Thomas. Married Eleanor Radcliffe,
    September 13, 1746
Thornberry, Ann. Daughter of William and
    Elizabeth, born April 9, 1747
Tolson, Mary. The wife of Benjamin, died
    June 24, 1748
Thomson, Mary. Married Robert Pully,
    August 28, 1748
Tomison, James. Son of Simon and Barbara, born
    July 8, 1748
Tomison, Elizabeth. Daughter of Simon, died
    September 8, 1748
Tomison, Jean. Departed this life,
    September 14, 1748

OVERWHARTON PARISH REGISTER.   173

Threlkeld, Henry. Married Mary Hinson,
November 2, 1748
Tyler, Anne. Daughter of Henry and Else, baptized
January 30, 1749
Turnham, John. Son of Thomas and Eleanor, born
May 3, 1749
Traverse, Rawleigh. Departed this life,
October 15, 1749
Towngate, Hannah. Was born in Prince William
County, January 9, 1750
Tifer, Jannet. Died at Morris Lynaugh's,
May 9, 1750
Toby, Thomas. Son of John and Elizabeth, born
January 20, 1751
Tongate, Jeremiah. Married Elizabeth Waus,
March 3, 1751
Tyler, Mary. Daughter of Henry and Alice, baptized
March 20, 1751
Tomison, Barbara. Wife of Simon, died
August 19, 1751
Tolson, Benjamin, Jr. Married Hannah
Maccothough, December 31, 1751
Todd, Nanny. Daughter of William and Margaret,
born October 13, 1752
Todd, William. Married Margaret Cocklen,
October 23, 1752

Tolson, Mary. Daughter of Benjamin and Hannah,
    born February 19, 1753
Thomson, John Clement. Son of Jean, born
    February 13, 1753
Toby, John. Son of John, born July 3, 1753
Toby, John. Son of John, died, February 3, 1754
Tolson, Ann. Married Isaac Dunnaway,
    May 25, 1754
Turner, Betty. Married Henry Dawson,
    December 15, 1754
Ticer, William. Married Aggy Hutt,
    December 15, 1754
Toby, Mary. Daughter of John and Elizabeth, born
    July 28, 1755
Tolson, Peggy. Was baptized September 2, 1755
Taylor, John. Married Elizabeth Summers,
    November 8, 1755
Taylor, Alexander. Married Hannah Brooke,
    February 24, 1757
Taylor, Philadelphia. Daughter of John, born
    February 2, 1757
Turner, James. Married Mary Matthews,
    March 3, 1757
Thomas, Jane. Married Feanly McCoy, July 18, 1757
Tolson, Nanny. Daughter of Benjamin and Hannah,
    born December 4, 1757

U.

V.

Voucheart, John. Son of William, born
October 21, 1752
Voucheart, John. Was baptized December 10, 1752
Vant, Franky. Daughter of James and Margaret, born
May 15, 1758

W.

Williams, Nathaniel. Son of George and Jean, born
October 5, 1730.
Williams, Margaret. Daughter of George and Jean,
born April 17, 1732
Williams, Benjamin. Son of George and Jean, born
June 14, 1734
Wright, John. Son of William and Rosamond, born
August 3, 1735
Williams, George. Son of George and Jean, born
August 21, 1736
Wright, Betty. Daughter of William and Rosamond,
born September 10, 1737
Wine, Richard. Married Anne Harvie, July 23, 1738

Waugh, William. Married Margaret Tyler,
                                September 10, 1738
Wells, Carty. Married Elizabeth Onsby,
                                September 28, 1738
Waters, Thomas. Married Catharine Hays,
                                September 28, 1738
Waters, Margaret. Daughter of Edward and
                                Catharine, January 25, 1739
Waugh, Tyler. Son of William and Margaret, born
                                February 29, 1739
Waters, Philmen. Son of Thomas, born
                                March 22, 1739
Williams, John Pope. Son of George and Jean, born
                                July 27, 1739
Whealy, James. Married Hannah Higgerson,
                                July 8, 1739
Whitecotton, Mary. Daughter of George and
                                Bridget, born January 20, 1739
Whitson, Margaret. Married Nicholas George,
                                December 25, 1740
Whitson, William. Son of William and Margaret,
                                born March 11, 1741
Wright, Constance. Daughter of William and
                                Rosamond, September 7, 1739
Welch, Margaret. Married John Prim,
                                September 9, 1739

OVERWHARTON PARISH REGISTER. 177

Wells, Sarah. Daughter of Carty and Elizabeth, born
October 10, 1739
Waters, James. Son of Thomas and Mary, born
October 25, 1739
Waller, Hannah. Daughter of George and Elizabeth,
born October 12, 1739
Wells, Charles. Son of Charles and Mary, born
January 10, 1740
Waugh, Elizabeth. Daughter of Joseph and Millon,
born March 31, 1740
Waugh. Mary. Married Alexander Doniphon,
June 17, 1740
Williams, Mary. Died at Charles Turner's,
June 20, 1740
Waugh, James. Married Betty French,
August 22, 1740
Wilkinson, William. Married Sarah Heffermot,
August 21, 1740
Wine, Mary. Daughter of Richard and Anne, born
October 1, 1740
Waller, William. Son of Edward and Anne, born
November 26, 1740
Wiot, Edmond. Son of Daniel and Susannah, born
October 1, 1740
Williams, Joseph. Married Mary Mallaken,
February 9, 1741

Withers, Elizabeth. Daughter of John and Hannah, born February 8, 1741

Wood, Archibald. Son of John and Tabitha, born April 15, 1741

Wells, Sarah. Daughter of Carty, died April 13, 1741

Wilkinson, John. Son of William, born July 6, 1741

Waugh, John. Son of James and Betty, born October 20, 1741

Wells, Isabel. Daughter of Carty and Elizabeth, born October 31, 1741

Waugh, Priscilla. Daughter of William and Margaret, born October 22, 1741

Waller, Margaret. Daughter of Charles and Elizabeth, born November 27, 1741

Whitecotton, Lettie and Jean. Daughters of Sarah, born November 14, 1741

Wiot, William. Son of Edmund and ———, born November 20, 1741

Williams, Jesse. Son of George and Jean, born December 21, 1741

Wade, Rachel. Married John McGuirk, December 25, 1741

Webster, Edmund. Married Margery Stanley, November 20, 1741

Whitson, William. Son of Samuel and Nan, born January 29, 1742

OVERWHARTON PARISH REGISTER.   179

Williams, George.   Son of Joseph, born
January 19, 1742
Waller, John.   Son of Edward and Anne, born
April 7, 1742
Whitson, Charles.   Son of William and Margaret,
born March 5, 1742
Watson, Andrew.   Married Mary Moses,
September 26, 1742
Wright, Windfield.   Son of William and Rose, born
March 22, 1742
Waters, Anne.   Daughter of Edward and Catharine,
born January 1, 1742
Wells, John.   Son of Charles and Mary, born
July 3, 1742
West, James.   Son of John, born September 26, 1742
Wine, Benjamin.   Son of Richard and Anne, born
December 19, 1742
Warner, Margaret.   Married James Dillon,
November 6, 1742
Wise, John.   Son of John and Mary, born
October 6, 1742
Wise, Elizabeth.   Married Patrick Roath,
October 9, 1742
Waugh, John.   Departed this life, November 17, 1742
Waugh, Traverse.   Son of Joseph William, born
January 24, 1743

180 OVERWHARTON PARISH REGISTER.

Withers, Bridget. Married William Allen,
February 15, 1743
Withers, Margaret. Daughter of John and Hannah,
born February 8, 1743
Webster, Anne. Married George Reaves, April 3, 1743
West, Carty. Daughter of Thomas and Catharine,
born March 12, 1743
Watson, John. Son of Elizabeth, born
January 27, 1743
Waters, Mary. Married John Shaw, June 12, 1743
Waters, John. Married Elizabeth Higgerson,
June 3, 1743
White, George. Married Anne Doniphan,
August 4, 1743
Wells, George. Son of Carty and Elizabeth, born
November 18, 1743
Whitcomb, John. Married Elizabeth Simpson,
November 24, 1743
Whitson, James. Son of William and Margaret, born
February 10, 1744
Whitson, Mary. Daughter of Samuel and Ann, born
April 19, 1744
Whitecotton, George. Departed this life,
March 23, 1744
Want, Sarah. Married William Corbin,
August 2, 1744

Whitcomb, Mary. Daughter of John, born
August 29, 1744
Withers, Wilmouth. Died at William Mathews,
August 21, 1744
Waller, Margaret. Daughter of George, born
July 27, 1744
Waugh, Sarah. Daughter of Betty and James,
baptized June 20, 1744
Walker, William. Married Elizabeth Monk,
May 23, 1744
Wells, Peyton. Son of Charles, born
Sepember 9, 1744
Withers, Ann. Married Henry Manzey,
November 11, 1744
Whitson, Elizabeth. Married George Green,
December 23, 1744
Whitson, Mary. Departed this life, January 25, 1745
Withers, Mary. Daughter of John and Hannah, born
January 22, 1745
Waters, Edward. Departed this life, February 2, 1745
West, Dorothy. Married Lawrence Suddeth,
April 18, 1745
Wine, Richard. Son of Richard and Ann, born
February 14, 1745
Wilkerson, John. Son of William, died
March 10, 1745

OVERWHARTON PARISH REGISTER.

Williams, Charles. Son of George and Jane, born
                                May 1, 1745
Whitson, Sarah. Married John Nelson,
                                December 7, 1745
Whalebone, Duke. Married Elizabeth Powell,
                                December 3, 1745
Whitson, Mary   Married William George,
                                November 1, 1745
Wood, Ann. Daughter of Thomas and Margaret,
                                born September 18, 1745
Waller, Charles. Son of Edward and Ann, born
                                January 27, 1746
Williams, Margaret. Married John Ball,
                                January 2, 1746
Waugh, James. Son of James and Elizabeth, born
                                February 4, 1746
West, James. Son of Thomas and Catharine, born
                                February 10, 1746
Whitcomb, Richard. Departed this life,
                                February 7, 1746
Withers, James. Departed this life in the 66th year of
                                his age, June 3, 1746
Whitson, Ann. Daughter of Ann, born June 17, 1746
Wheeler, John. Departed this life, August 5, 1746
Waller, Jeany. Daughter of George and Elizabeth,
                                born July 28, 1746

OVERWHARTON PARISH REGISTER. 183

Wise, Samuel. Son of John, born July 15, 1746
Waller, Elizabeth. Was baptized September 7, 1746
Waugh, James. Son of James and Betty, died
September 3, 1746
Whalebone, Thomas. Son of Duke and Elizabeth,
born September 4, 1746
Wiggonton, Peter. Married Winefred Eaves,
October 13, 1746
Weeks, Anny. Married Edward Proctor,
February 15, 1747
Wells, Eleanor. Daughter of Charles, born
April 19, 1747
Walker, Elizabeth. Daughter of William and
Elizabeth, born April 3, 1747
Withers, William. Son of John and Hannah, born
March 21, 1747
Wiggonton, Anne. Died at home,
November 22, 1747
Waugh, Betty. Daughter of James and Betty, born
September 4, 1747
Waugh, Betty. Departed this life,
September 14, 1747
Waters, Diana. Daughter of Thomas and Mary, born
November 5, 1747
Whitecotton, Bridget. Married William McConchie,
November 10, 1747

184   *OVERWHARTON PARISH REGISTER.*

White, Mary.   Daughter of George and Ann, born
September 9, 1747
White, Rosamond.   Departed this life,
February 19, 1748
Wright, Jane.   Married Richard Nowland,
December 26, 1747
Withers, Keene.   Married Elizabeth Cave,
December 21, 1747
Waugh, Joseph.   Died September 4, 1747
Wine, Richard.   Had two children born September 2, 1747, one of them died September 28, 1748
Weddall, Thomas.   Married Isabel Robe,
January, 3, 1748
White, Rosamond.   Departed this life,
February 19, 1748
Waller, Ann.   Wife of Edward, died February 29, 1748
Waller, Edward.   Son of Edward, born
February 27, 1748
Weathers, Susannah.   Daughter of John and Judy,
born February 1, 1748
Whitecotton, Axton.   Son of Husband Foot, born
February 3, 1748
Wood, Lizzie.   Daughter of Thomas and Margaret,
born March 18, 1748
Waugh, Solomon.   Married Betty Chinn,
April 13, 1748

OVERWHARTON PARISH REGISTER. 185

Waters, Diana, Daughter of Thomas, died
May 27, 1748
Waller, John. Son of Edward, died June 6, 1748
Waller, Susannah. Departed this life,
October 18, 1748
Wilson, John. Married Ann Asberry, August 16, 1748
Weathers, Susannah. Daughter of Judy, died
October 9, 1748
Waters, Jean. Married John Monslow,
October 26, 1748
Withers, Ann. Daughter of Cain and Betty, baptized
December 4, 1748
Wingfield, Owen. Married Mary Hurst,
November 26, 1748
Wood, Lizzie. Daughter of Thomas and Margaret,
died November 13, 1748
Waugh, Mieajiah. Son of Solomon and Elizabeth,
born January 9, 1749
Withers, Thomas. Son of John and Hannah, born
January 15, 1749
Williams, William. Son of Jean, born
January 26, 1749
White, Joseph. Married Elizabeth Gill,
January 31, 1749
Webster, Barbara. Married William Groves,
February 2, 1749

Wiggonton, William. Son of Peter and Winefred,
born May 29, 1749
Whitcomb, Margaret. Daughter of John and
Elizabeth, born August 16, 1749
Weathers, Nancy. Daughter of John and Judith,
born July 1, 1749
Whitcomb, Mary. Died at Richard Wine's,
April 23, 1751
Whalebone, Nanny. Daughter of Duke and
Elizabeth, born October 5, 1749
White, Alice. Daughter of Joseph and Elizabeth,
born December 18, 1749
Weathers, Ann. Daughter of Ann and Thomas, born
December 10, 1749
Wine, Peggy. Daughter of Richard and Ann, born
December 2, 1749
Waller, Charles. Died at John Waugh's,
December 4, 1749
Walker, Mary. Daughter of William and Elizabeth,
born January 9, 1750
Wilson, Ann. Died at John Dayton's,
December 31, 1749
Wiggonton, Jane. Married Moses Bland,
January 14, 1750
Wells, Eleanor. Daughter of Carty, born
February 21, 1750

OVERWHARTON PARISH REGISTER. 187

Williams, George. Departed this life,
February 12, 1750
Wilson, Mary,   Died at William Lunsford's,
March 9, 1750
Wood, Thomas. Departed this life, February 8, 1750
Whitson, Jess. Son of William and Margaret, born
May 8, 1750
Wood, Elizabeth. Daughter of Thomas and Margaret,
born April 29, 1750
Waugh, Captain James. Departed this life,
May 9, 1750
Weathers, Samuel. Departed this life, June 30, 1750
Wawal, Charles. Married Mary Hall,
November 16, 1751
Weathers, Elizabeth Blufard. Mother of Thomas,
died August 13, 1750
Wilson, Spencer. Son of John and Ann, born
August 30, 1750
White, Alexander. Son of George and Ann, born
August 11, 1750
Waters, William. Married Jean Cash, April 6, 1751
Wiggonton, Henry. Married Margaret Bridwell,
November 12, 1750
Wans, Elizabeth. Married Jeremiah Lungate,
March 3, 1751
Waller, John. Married Mary Mathews, July 4, 1751

Waller, Ann. Married Thomas Bailly,
                                July 10, 1751
Waugh, Betty. Married Andrew Edwards,
                                May 7, 1751
Wells, Benjamin. Son of Charles and Mary, born
                                August 22, 1751
Whitson, Elizabeth. Married Benjamin
                      MacCollough, December 17, 1751
Waller, William. Son of John and Mary, born
                                December 24, 1751
Waller, Elizabeth. Married John Peyton,
                                November 17, 1751
Winlock, Elizabeth. Daughter of Joseph and
                      Margaret, born April 12, 1752
Whitcomb, Eliza. Daughter of John, born
                                February 26, 1752
Wilson, Nanny. Daughter of John, born
                                February 25, 1752
Wilson, John. Married Sarah Brooks,
                                February 7, 1752
Weathers, John. Son of John and Judith, born
                                March 14, 1752
Waters, Mary. Married John Fitzpatrick,
                                February 12, 1752
Washington, William. Son of Baily and Catharine,
                                born February 28, 1752

Weathers, Joel. Son of Thomas and Ann, born
February 7, 1752
Walker, Margaret. Daughter of William and
Elizabeth, baptized May 1, 1752
Withers, James. Son of Keene, born May 9, 1752
Wiggonton, Peter. Son of Peter and Winney, born
September 17, 1752
West, Edward. Married Elizabeth Mills,
October 6, 1752
Waller, Mary. Married Edward Kendon,
April 15, 1753
Wren, James. Married Catharine Brent,
March 27, 1753
Wright, Rosamond. Wife of William, died
March 16, 1753
Waugh, David. Died at Priscilla Hayes',
March 22, 1753
Withers, George. Son of John and Hannah, born
February 2, 1753
White, Thomas. Was baptized May 3, 1753
Waller, Theodosia. Daughter of George, baptized
April 1, 1753
Waters, Jean. Daughter of Charles and Hannah,
born June 28, 1753
Wilson, Hannah. Daughter of John, born
June 16, 1753

Waller, Sarah. Daughter of John and Mary, born
                                    June 12, 1753
Waller, Edward. Departed this life suddenly,
                                November 20, 1753
Washington, Bailey. Son af Bailey, born
                                December 12, 1753
Wright, William. Married Mary Brent,
                                 October 18, 1753
White, Ann. Daughter of Ann and George, born
                                 January 14, 1754
Withers, William. Son of Keene and Elizabeth,
                                February 20, 1754
Williams, Elizabeth. Married John Gill,
                                   March 3, 1754
Waters, James. Son of William and Jane, born
                                    May 26, 1754
White, Alice. Daughter of Joseph and Elizabeth,
                            died August 13, 1754
Waller, Mary. Married George Dabney,
                               September 11, 1754
Withers, Hannah. Daughter of John and Hannah,
                           born September 8, 1754
Waller, Milly. Daughter of Charles, died
                                  January 7, 1755
Winlock, Sarah. Daughter of Joseph and Margaret,
                            born February 10, 1755

OVERWHARTON PARISH REGISTER. 191

West, William Mills. Son of Edward and Elizabeth,
born March 29, 1755
Wilson, John. Son of John and Ann, born
March 25, 1755
Woodward, Jenny. Daughter of William and
Hannah, born August 10, 1755
Wilson, Else. Daughter of John and Ann, born
May 16, 1757
Wren, James. Son of Catharine, baptized
December 21, 1758
Waller, Edward. Son of John and Mary, born
December 10, 1755
Wiggonton, James. Son of Peter and Winefred, died
February 10, 1755
Withers, John. Son of Cain, born
February 23, 1756
Williams, Mary Ann. Married Thomas Smith,
February 21, 1756
Wheeler, Eleanor. Married William Edwards,
February 12, 1756
Wiggonton, James. Married Sarah Botts,
February 9, 1756
Wheeler, Martha. Married William Howard,
April 25, 1756
Withers, Mary Ann. Daughter of Thomas and Ann,
born, April 19, 1756

192 OVERWHARTON PARISH REGISTER.

Washington, John. Son of Bailey and Catharine,
 born May 5, 1756
Wiggonton, Nancy. Daughter of James and Sarah,
 born November 8, 1756
Waters, Mark. Married Ann Harding, July 20, 1756
Washington, Robert. Married Alice Strother,
 December 16, 1756
Willamson, James. Married Susannah Weyton,
 November 4, 1756
Withers, Ann. Daughter of John and Hannah, born
 November 9, 1756
Weyton, Susannah. Married James Williamson,
 November 4, 1756
Wall, Margaret. A poor parisioner, died
 April 7, 1757
Waters, Virginia. Married Richard Fristoe,
 February 28, 1757
Wiggonton, James. Son of Peter and Winney, born
 February 24, 1757
Weathers, Eleanor. Daughter of John and Judith,
 born January 15, 1757
Wilson, Else. Was baptized August 25, 1757
Withers, James. Married Sukey Waller,
 December 7, 1757
Waller, Sukey. Married James Withers,
 December 7, 1757

OVERWHARTON PARISH REGISTER.   193

Welit, Elizabeth.   Married John Smith,
December 7, 1757
White, Ann.   Died at Edward Templeman's,
December 13, 1757
Weathers, Ann.   Wife of Thomas, died
October 13, 1757
Weathers, Jean and Ann.   Daughters of Thomas and Ann, born October 13, 1757
Winlock, Joseph.   Son of Joseph and Margaret, born
May 11, 1758
Washington, Elizabeth.   Daughter of Catharine and Bailey, born March 16, 1758
Withers, Elizabeth.   Married Andrew Edwards,
January 19, 1758
Waller, John.   Son of John and Mary, born
December 27, 1758

X.

Y.

Young, Margaret.   Married John Humphreys, Jr.,
September 23, 1738
Young, William.   Married Patience Sinclair,
July 23, 1744

Young, Robert. Son of William and Patience, born
                                                    May 30, 1745
Young, Robert. Son of William, died
                                                    October 1, 1745
Yelton, James. Married Isabell Hinson,
                                                    November 13, 1743
Yelton, Charles. Son of James and Isabell, born
                                                    November 1, 1746
Young, Richard. Married Elizabeth Green,
                                                    December 27, 1746
Young, Sarah. Daughter of William and Patience,
                                                    born April 1, 1747
Yelton, James. Son of James and Isabell, born
                                                    July 15, 1749
Young, John. Departed this life at William Kirke's
                                                    March 11, 1752
Yelton, Mary. Daughter of James and Isabell, born
                                                    April 18, 1752
Yelton, Ann. Daughter of James and Isabell, born
                                                    July 26, 1755
Yates, Elizabeth. Married ———, February 4, 1758

Z.

This Register was brought to William Moncure's residence in the year 1825 by his son, William R. Moncure, who was a great grandson of the Rev. John Moncure, Minister of Overwharton Parish, and was recently found among the papers of Judge R. C. L. Moncure, by his executor, Powhatan Moncure, Stafford County, Virginia, and by me copied for Mr. Wm. F. Boogher, of Washington, D. C., and I hereby certify that from pages 1 to 194, inclusive, of this book contains a true copy, (including spelling,) of the Register of Overwharton Parish, Stafford County, Virginia, from 1720 to 1758 omitting only such items as refers to negroes.

POWHATAN MONCURE,
Custodian of Old Records of said Parish.
October 10, 1899.

www.ingramcontent.com/pod-product-compliance
Lightning Source LLC
Chambersburg PA
CBHW051058230426
43667CB00013B/2351